THE
AMERICAN
AUTOMOBILE

THE
AMERICAN
AUTOMOBILE

TONY BEADLE
with IAN PENBERTHY

a Salamander book

Salamander Books Ltd
LONDON

A SALAMANDER BOOK

Published by Salamander Books Ltd
129-137 York Way, London N7 9LG
United Kingdom

© Salamander Books Ltd, 1996

This edition published in 1996 by
SMITHMARK Publishers,
a division of U. S. Media Holdings, Inc.,
16 East 32nd Street,
New York, NY 10016

9 8 7 6 5 4 3 2 1

SMITHMARK books are available for bulk
purchase for sales promotion and premium
usage. For details write or call the manager of
special sales,
SMITHMARK Publishers, 16 East 32nd Street,
New York, NY 10016; (212) 532-6600

ISBN 0-8317-6267-5

All correspondence concerning the content of
this volume should be addressed to
Salamander Books Ltd.

CREDITS
Managing Editor: Joanna Smith
Editor: Helen Stone
Art Editor: Paul Johnson
Picture Research: Ian Penberthy
Original Design Concept: Aardvark Design
    Studio Ltd
Color Separation: P&W Graphics PTE Ltd
Printed in Italy

DEDICATION
This book is dedicated to my wife, Jennie, for
putting up with my grumpy behavior during the
final stages of putting together the text, and for
not moaning (too much!) about the lack of work
done around the house during the time spent
researching and writing.

ACKNOWLEDGEMENTS
Any book of this nature requires an incredible
amount of help from a number of people and
sadly, it isn't possible to thank them all
individually. But I would like to express my
special thanks to co-author Ian Penberthy for his
efforts, Joanna Smith for her unfailing good nature
and Richard Collins for getting the project off the
ground in the first place. I would also like to
acknowledge the following for their assistance:
Helen Jones Early of the Oldsmobile History
Center, Mike Key, Nicky Wright, Dan Lyons, Rod
Blackaller, Julian Balme and all the authors and
publishers of the numerous books and magazines
that provided invaluable reference material.

CONTENTS

INTRODUCTION

As any automotive writer will tell you, looking back can be filled with pitfalls. Often our vision of the past is distorted, just like peering through the double curvature of the wrap-around Panoramic windshield on a 1954 Oldsmobile Starfire – the images may be twisted out of shape or highlighted in sharp focus, or even slightly colored by the tint in the glass, according to our viewpoint. In some extreme cases the alterations are so dramatic that the picture we see becomes almost unrecognizable to people who were actually there at the time. Yet we all share a common desire to capture the true spirit of the period, as embodied in the designs of the cars – from the determination of the entrepreneurs who had the dream, to the stylists that created the form, the engineers that crafted the metal, the workers that assembled the components and the customers who drove the finished result – it's just that our perception of what's on the other side of that window through time takes on a different emphasis.

There is no other nation in the world where the automobile has become so much a part of the fabric of everyday life as the USA. And throughout its life, the automobile has faithfully mirrored the dreams, needs and wants of the American people – whether it was the basic black Tin Lizzie of Henry Ford, the majestic doomed splendor of a Marmon Sixteen, the outrageous fins and lavish chrome on a '59 Cadillac, the ground-shaking performance of a Dodge Hemi Challenger or the quirky sawn-off economy of the American Motors' Gremlin – they all represent a part of a fascinating story.

But it hasn't just reflected, the automobile has also exerted a tremendous influence on the way we behave, changed the way we think, caused huge physical changes to our surroundings, and molded the landscape. For the most part, the automobile has been a machine of great benefit to mankind. But it is more than a mere collection of nuts and bolts, the car can

interact with people like no other machine. Climbing behind the wheel makes you part of the machine, while retaining control of your ultimate destiny – barring poor navigation, traffic congestion, breakdowns and (heaven forbid) an accident or encounter with the highway patrol! It has given us fun, excitement, pleasure of ownership, a freedom of movement for the individual that nothing else can equal and provided work and a source of income for untold millions over the years. Oh sure, cars have been the cause of frustration, anger, misery, injury and death too, but in my opinion the good far outweighs the bad.

The variety of automobiles created during the period covered by this book is enormous, and the list of auto makers that have come and gone is also lengthy; to attempt to cover each one in detail would require more volumes than an encyclopedia. This was obvi-ously not possible, and the dedicated histori-an will note omissions, some more signficant than others but, in the end with limited space available, the selection process had to be ruthless and a choice exercised.

Included are obvious, well-known clas-sics, some popular favorites, plus others con-sidered to be of particular historical interest or having design features of note, and there are even a few relatively obscure cars that were regarded as simply too fascinating to be left out. This is by no means a definitive history of the American automobile, and was never intended to be so. It is a celebration of the best and the worst, some brilliant successes and some dismal flops, classic marques and bizarre oddities. Maybe this book might even inspire a few enquiring minds to undertake further research and uncover previously hid-den facts or information – if so, that would be an added bonus.

Tony Beadle
May 1996

Below: Surely there can have been few automobiles shaped more like a carapace than the 1949 Lincoln Cosmopolitan?

1919

World War One had ended in November 1918, the economy was experiencing a post-war mini-boom based on the euphoria of victory, and the population of Detroit was nearly four times what it was at the start of the century, thanks to the burgeoning business of building automobiles. At the heart of the Motor City's prosperity was the incredible ever-expanding empire of Henry Ford, based on the corner-stone of just one model – the Model T.

Arriving in October 1908, the Model T Ford was to revolutionize the automobile industry and help establish a freedom of movement for Americans – the car would come within reach of almost anyone. Eleven years on, the Model T was going strong and, if altered in appearance (it had a major facelift in 1917), no backwoods mechanic could fail to recognize the car or its components and know exactly how to fix whatever went wrong.

Mass production was the key to its phenomenal success, but equally important was Ford's insistence on reducing the price when possible, stimulating demand even more and creating further profits. When introduced, the Model T sold at $850, but by 1919 the 2-door Runabout was only $500. And while the first full year of production saw 17,771 put together, with the coming of the moving assembly line and its refinement of operation, in 1919 an amazing 820,455 cars bearing the Ford name were manufactured – almost double the previous year's output and nearly half the

Above: At just $500, the two-seat Runabout was the cheapest Model T on offer in 1919 and yet it was acceptable for use even on formal occasions. By this time Ford only offered cars in 'any color as long as it's black' but prior to 1914 Model Ts were painted in a number of hues.

Left: Prior to 1919, Willys-Overland was second to Ford in production, but a factory strike delayed a new model intended to combat the Model T. When it did arrive, it was priced at over $800 – way above the Ford – and could no longer compete. This Overland has just completed a seven day, non-stop publicity run in high gear.

total for the whole US auto industry. A further milestone reached in this year was the production of the three millionth Model T.

It is widely assumed that Ford could keep the price of the Model T so low because it was churned out, year after year, without any alterations. This isn't so. Changes were made all the time – models came and went, different suppliers were used and components were modified, either to cure problems or to provide a cheaper method of production.

But the original concept of a car for the masses remained and the specification was more or less constant. The engine was a four cylinder L-head of 176.7 cu.in. developing 20 horsepower, cooled by thermo-syphon action, coupled to a unique planetary transmission with two forward speeds and reverse and a multiple disc clutch, while a torque tube drive connected this to the rear axle. The wheelbase was 100 inches, wooden spoked wheels were 30 inches and suspension was by transverse semi-elliptic leaf springs.

Within that framework the Model T evolved bit by bit, and 1919 saw an electric starter and battery as standard on closed models and offered as an option on open cars. This in turn led to an instrument panel being fitted with a single gauge (an ammeter), ignition/light switch and choke knob – speedometers were installed by dealers or owners. Demountable rim wheels were also available for the first time to make tire changing easier.

The Model T became forever enshrined in American folklore for being virtually indestructible and, in spite of its quirky features, utterly reliable. Cheerfully used and savagely abused, it was a target of derision and affection in like amounts, at home on the remotest farm or in the teeming city, and it captured the heart of the nation in a manner that no other automobile in history – before or since – has come close to equaling.

Left: Chevrolet was started by William C. Durant with the intention of building a 'light car' at an affordable price, and had enjoyed some considerable success after a rather hesitant start, enabling Durant to regain control of General Motors in September 1915. But by 1919, Chevy's offerings had grown heavier and more expensive. Typical of the period is this Series 490 4-door sedan (Chevrolet's first closed model) which included standard equipment like a speedometer, ammeter, demountable wheel rims, tire pump and electric horn, among other things, all for a cost of $1185.

1920

Choosing a suitable name for a new car company must have been a vexing task for the hundreds of so-called entrepreneurs in the Twenties, as proposing to set up an automobile producing business had been a lucrative method of selling stock and raising millions of dollars to fund the business since the turn of the century. Spurred on by the successes of people like Ransom E. Olds (Oldsmobile and Reo), William C. Durant (Buick, Chevrolet and General Motors), Henry Ford and many others in making personal fortunes out of the fledgling auto industry, the crooked speculators took full advantage of the boom and the naivety of investors. The ReVere is just one of many automotive enterprises that, for one reason or another, failed to last the distance.

During this frantic time, almost every name that would look good at the head of a certificate had been used (some more than once) and the names of US automobile companies registered run the whole gamut of the alphabet, from Abbott-Akin to Zip (both of whom, coincidentally, didn't survive 1914). Yet it is surprising to find only one make of car named after the famous Revolutionary War figure Paul Revere.

When Revere made his epic ride in 1775 to warn the Massachusetts militia men that British troops were advancing on Concord, the 20 mile night time journey from Boston was regarded as an incredible adventure and rightly so. How the patriotic hero and erstwhile silversmith, engraver and dentist would have viewed a motorcar bearing his image is impossible to say, and it seems odd that when the ReVere (that's how the name was usually depicted) did appear, it was to come from the Mid-West, rather than his New England home.

The ReVere Motor Car Corporation was established in Logansport, Indiana in 1917 to begin construction of an automobile using the race-bred, four cylinder Duesenberg engine. Two of the three company's principals came from racing backgrounds – Gil Anderson had driven successfully for Stutz, while Tom Mooney had been part of the Premier team. The third, Adolph Monsen, previously owned and operated a garage in Chicago and built a few cars as part of that business, but on a strictly limited basis.

The choice of powerplant was indicative that the trio were not aiming the ReVere at the

Model T market, but the stylish and sporty (and expensive) end of the spectrum. And so when the first cars were completed in 1918, they turned out to be high priced as well as high performance. The ReVere would ultimately achieve its main recognition for its speedster models – also called raceabouts, runabouts and roadsters by other manufacturers – for which there was quite a fashion in the early Twenties, but the initial offerings also included an open touring car and a Victoria.

In dividing the workload, it was Anderson who was chiefly responsible for the chassis development, with the suspension including outboard semi-elliptic rear leaf springs and (advanced for the period) provision for shock absorbers. Monsen took care of the engine, making some modifications and, in due course, producing his own version of the Rochester-Duesenberg four cylinder motor.

Right: Despite being described by a sales slogan as "America's Incomparable Car" the fact that the ReVere failed to survive the Twenties was due more to the mishandling of financial matters than any shortcomings of the cars themselves.

Mooney's role is less clear, but he evidently helped out in various different capacities.

The ReVere promotional blurb was fulsome enough: "The last word in classy design built by people who know, for people who want the classiest..." and the company adopted the slogan "America's Incomparable Car". A publicity stunt saw famed racing ace, Cannon Ball Baker, drive a ReVere tourer around the USA in 1918, clocking up over 16,000 miles and the ReVere was also exhibited at several major auto shows generating a fair amount of attention for the marque.

Production had commenced in earnest at the start of 1919, and the ReVere carried a hefty price tag of around $3,850 from the factory – about ten times the cost of the cheapest Model T Ford! The company soon began to receive orders for specially-built cars for heads of state of foreign countries, one of the most prestigious being King Alfonso XIII of Spain who took delivery of a Victoria model.

Outwardly, the ReVere automobile venture seemed to be progressing nicely but, behind the scenes, things were less satisfactory. Financial control of the company was in the hands of a quartet headed by president Newton Van Zandt, and aided by vice-president A. A. Seagraves, treasurer C. H. Wilson and secretary E. R. Mattingly. ReVere stock was being sold in large quantities, no doubt

Above: The 1920 Packard Twin Six. This was the world's first 12 cylinder car manufactured in series quantity with over 35,000 built between 1916 and 1923. Its 60° L-head V12 of 424 cu.in engine produced 90bhp.

due to a concocted prospectus statement that a contract for the next five years of production had been agreed with an Eastern syndicate, guaranteeing a profit of $500 on every car made and amounting to a total of $45 million which attracted plenty of eager investors.

But there was no such contract, and matters quickly started to go wrong. In December 1920, ReVere was petitioned into bankruptcy by three creditors from Chicago and the court action dragged on into 1921. Then, in August of that year, Van Zandt was sued for grand lar-

cency by a stockholder from Buffalo, New York, but the ReVere president was acquitted of the charge. Further investigations into the company's affairs precipitated its failure, and in November 1922 the factory was sold off.

However, that wasn't the end of the ReVere. By February 1923, a reorganization had taken place and the ReVere Motor Company was born, with Adolph Monsen taking up the post of vice-president and general manager. Manufacture of sedans and roadsters continued through 1924 using the Monsen derivation of the Duesenberg engine, and then in 1925 a Continental six cylinder was introduced as well.

All was not well at ReVere though for, despite the new organisational structure, the company's image and reputation never really recovered from the earlier financial scandal. Finally, in 1926, the factory closed its doors forever and the marque named after an American hero disappeared.

Prior to its departure, the last ReVere models offered balloon tires, four wheel brakes and a rudimentary form of power steering. This unusual system comprised of two steering wheels, one inside the other, which had a lower ratio to make it easier to park, but the idea died with the ReVere company.

At it's peak in 1920, the ReVere represented all that was both good and bad in the auto industry of the time. In the speedster ranks, it never quite rivaled the leading makers' models like the Mercer Raceabout and the Stutz Bearcat, although it was on a par with other less well-known marques such as Biddle,

Kissel, Marmon and Paige, but the financial wranglings of the company rather than any mechanical shortcomings were its undoing.

It was the beginning of the Jazz Age – an era of fads and freakish fashions that came and went with amazing rapidity and, despite a depressed US economy in 1920-21, a feeling of prosperity prevailed. Prohibition started on January 16, 1920, and the Chicago White Sox were accused of throwing the World Series, but politicians were fueling the consumer culture by promising "a car in every garage" and there were now around 9 million automobiles in the USA as motoring was becoming more a part of daily life rather than just a frivolous pastime for the rich.

Above: The Essex debuted in 1919, and in August 1920, set a new record carrying mail from San Francisco to New York in 4 days, 14 hours, and 43 minutes.

Below: Gaston Chevrolet won the 1920 Indy 500 at an average speed of 88.62mph in a Frontenac, built by his brother Louis after he had left the Chevrolet Motor Company following a dispute with William C. Durant in 1914. After that, none of the Swiss-born Chevrolet brothers would have any connection with the marque that bore their name.

1921

Proof of the rapid development of the automobile's place at the very heart of the American way of life is shown from several incidents during this year. Warren G. Harding became the first US president to travel to his inauguration in a car – a Packard Twin Six, and, at the other end of the scale, was another first – the Pig Stand, a drive-in restaurant in Dallas, Texas, where barbecued pork sandwiches were served to people to eat in their cars. Meanwhile, in an effort to regulate the ever-increasing flow of cars on the streets, the Detroit police were experimenting with synchronized traffic lights, having introduced the three-colored light two years earlier.

But the economy was still depressed at the start of the year, with 5 million people unemployed. As Ford slashed the price of the Model T to stimulate demand, grabbing over 60% of the market, the need for cheaper cars was recognized by other manufacturers. Oldsmobile had established itself as a builder of medium-priced, good quality automobiles, but reacted to the down-turn in sales by bringing out a four cylinder car – the Model 43-A. Since 1916, Oldsmobiles had all been powered by either a six or eight cylinder engine and the four was a welcome addition.

At under $1400, the 43-A was the cheapest Oldsmobile by a wide margin (their eight cylinder models cost nearly twice as much), yet they couldn't hope to approach the rock-bottom prices set by Ford. A Model T Runabout eventually sunk to $325 in 1921, but a 2-door sedan was $760 – still half the price of the new Olds. The difference in price is reflected in the annual production. While Ford churned out nearly 1.3 million cars, Oldsmobile's output was a modest 19,157, of which 13,867 were the Model 43-A.

Above: 1921 saw the arrival of Henry Leland's new V8 Lincoln, but although superbly engineered, the conservatively-styled luxury cars from the creator of Cadillac struggled to survive in what were difficult times and the company went into liquidation in November. Henry Ford bought Lincoln in February 1922 and thereby ensured the future of the marque.

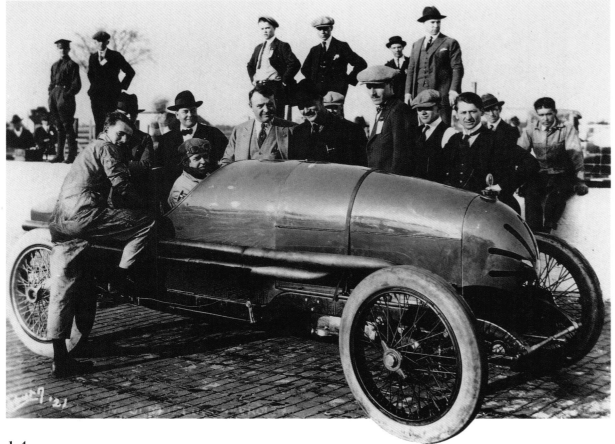

Left: A Frontenac again took the chequered flag at the Indianapolis 500 Mile Race, this time with Tommy Milton behind the wheel. His winning average speed was 89.62mph.

14

Despite the reduction in price compared to earlier models, the four cylinder Oldsmobile remained a quality automobile, far more sophisticated and better equipped than the Ford. While the cheaper open models were more popular, the Olds 4-door sedan looked more in keeping with the times, sporting the fashionable sloping windshield, but all featured smoother body work lines, especially where the hood joined the passenger compartment.

Mechanically too, the Oldsmobile was in a higher class, with its 224 cu.in. engine putting out 43 horsepower, over double that of the Ford four. And, featuring a simple manual transmission with a single plate, dry disc clutch, torque tube drive and spiral bevel gear rear axle, the Olds was as conventional as could be. Dimensionally, the Oldsmobile was also unremarkable, sitting on a wheelbase of 115 inches with 32 x 4 tires on wooden spoke artillery wheels. It all added up to a straightforward package that appealed to those drivers who wanted a little bit more from an automobile and were prepared to pay extra for it.

Oldsmobile might not have had the commanding presence in the market enjoyed by the overwhelming Ford juggernaut but, as a small part of the complex General Motors organisation put together by Billy Durant, it would survive and prosper. Pierre du Pont had taken over as president of GM, but it was Alfred P. Sloan who directed the essential rationalization programme needed to unravel the mess created by Durant. Part of the restructuring meant a clearer definition of the market levels in which each marque sold its products and it was decided that Oldsmobile's future was to be with bigger and better automobiles. As a consequence, the four would be discarded after 1923 and, thereafter, the Olds would use only six and eight cylinder engines.

Below: Although the cheaper open cars were more popular, this Oldsmobile 4-door sedan exhibits some of the fashionable trends in automobile design of the early Twenties, in particular the sloping windshield, which was also used by many other manufacturers.

1922

As we stand on the brink of the 21st century, it seems possible that the electric car will become a significant part of daily transport in the future, yet at one period it was the most favored method of automobile propulsion. The reasons for this were obvious – the electric car was clean, ran smoothly and quietly and didn't require the vigorous hand cranking of the gasoline engine or the firing of a steam boiler to get it started in the morning.

Electric power was also a familiar technology, with Thomas Edison having introduced electric lighting to New York in 1881, and most large cities had electric streetcars, whereas the gasoline engine was still in its infancy and suffered from plenty of teething troubles. The downside was that electric vehicles were expensive, heavy, and had a limited range before the batteries needed recharging.

For city use, however, the electric car was unsurpassed and became extremely popular with the wives of the wealthy, even indicating a certain social status and, at one time, there were many makes available to the discerning buyer. One of the more famous of these was Rauch & Lang. Formed as a carriage building company in Cleveland, Ohio, in 1884, Rauch & Lang entered the automobile business in 1903 by taking on an agency for the Buffalo Electric car. The first Rauch & Lang electric followed in 1905 and things progressed from there, the marque establishing itself as a supplier of quality automobiles. One of the largest electrics ever made was the 1912 Rauch & Lang six passenger town car which cost $3,800.

Sales of electric cars, or 'juicers' as they were sometimes called, peaked in 1914 with 4,669 units. These were mostly elegant carriages, very tall, with large areas of glass and plush interiors. The major problem with the electric car was battery life and this is still true today. Although a range of between 30 and 75 miles was possible, depending on the speed driven, overnight recharging was necessary which meant plugging in to special equipment in the owner's garage. Another disadvantage was the sheer weight of the batteries, around 1,000 pounds on an average car, which slowed acceleration somewhat. In addition, the batteries generally needed replacing after about three years and this also proved expensive.

All Rauch & Lang electric cars were similar in appearance. With no need for a radiator, they had a rounded-off nose and almost all had a very upright stance and a virtually flat roof with sharp corners. This design was common to almost all electric cars of this period. But travel horizons were expanding and, whereas a top speed of 20mph and a range of under fifty miles was fine for local journeys, long distance trips were another matter. Lengthy promotional journeys were mounted by electric car manufacturers to counteract these shortcomings, and a Detroit Electric even managed to exceed 200 miles between charges on one trip, but the need for more frequent recharging remained the norm.

Below: Electric cars were much favored for city use because of their smooth running and silent operation. Rauch & Lang were one of the most successful builders of electrics, but turned to taxis as the market went into decline and the gasoline engine took over. The rounded nose and upright style were typical features of most electric cars of this period.

By 1919, the market for electric cars was in decline, mainly due to improvements in the gasoline engine and the wider availability of the self-starter. Even so, Rauch & Lang were still producing 700 cars a year. In 1920 the passenger car part of the business was sold to the Stevens-Duryea organization and moved to Chicopee Falls, Massachusetts.

In 1922, Rauch & Lang Inc (as the new company was called) started producing electric powered taxi cabs, and this seems to have been the mainstay of production for the few remaining years of the business, which closed in 1928. Towards the end they were building as many, if not more, gasoline powered taxis as they were electric cars.

Above: Between 1915 and 1924, the Dort Motor Car Company of Flint, Michigan, turned out over 107,000 automobiles. J. Dallas Dort together with his chief engineer, Etienne Planche, was responsible for a succession of good cars, such as this 1922 coupe powered by a 30hp Lycoming four cylinder engine.

1923

Whenever steam-powered cars are mentioned, the name Stanley springs to mind, so it is somewhat startling to note that during the early years of this century, there were over 100 successful companies building steam vehicles in the USA.

However, it is the Stanley Steamer that is remembered above all others. Stanley was one of the more popular makes, lasted longer in the business than its rivals and is the only steam-powered machine to hold the World Land Speed Record (127.659mph over the flying mile at Daytona Beach in January 1906) – a remarkable feat.

Whilst operating a photographic equipment manufacturing company in Watertown, Massachusetts, identical twins, Francis E. and Freeland O. Stanley produced a highly effective steam car in 1898. After a demonstration, where the Stanley out-performed all other entrants on a hill climb contest, the brothers received orders for 200 cars.

Early in 1899, the Stanley factory was visited by John Brisbane Walker, a publisher, who liked what he saw and offered to buy the company. Having just got things off the ground, the Stanleys were reluctant to sell and put a huge price on their operation hoping to put Walker off. He agreed to pay the $250,000 asked and, in partnership with Amzi Lorenzo Barber, established the Locomobile car company building steamers to the Stanley design. Walker and Barber soon disagreed and Walker left to set up his own steam car production using the Mobile name. Walker's Mobile only lasted until 1903, and Locomobile switched exclusively to gasoline power the following year.

Meanwhile, having made a financial killing from their initial venture into auto building, the Stanley brothers had been busy developing an improved steam engine and formed the Stanley Motor Carriage Company in 1902. Litigation over patent infringements and breach of contract were overcome, and by 1912 over 5,000 Stanley steamers had been sold, the body design evolving into a rounded "coffin-nose" style concealing the front-mounted boiler, with the two cylinder engine driving directly on the rear axle.

Despite updates, such as condensors and flash boilers, the main drawback with steam power remained its slow warm-up time and, as gasoline engines improved, Stanley's sales

Above: Maxwell had combined with Chalmers in 1922, but the merger was in trouble, until Walter P. Chrylser arrived to sort things out in 1923. Engineering defects plagued Maxwell cars and it took a huge recall and free repairs to alleviate the situation. Refurbished '23 Maxwells were promoted as the "Good Maxwell" in an attempt to improve the marque's poor image, but by 1925, the Chrysler name superseded Maxwell and a dynasty was born. The 1923 Maxwell Club Coupe was powered by a 30hp four cylinder engine.

Right: To all intents, the Stanley Series 740 Tourer looks like a conventional automobile. The dummy radiator grille and filler cap hide the boiler, while the two cylinder steam engine drives directly on the rear axle. Although good performers with smooth running characteristics, steam-powered cars lost out to gasoline because of the inconvenience of the slow warm-up from cold. In 1923, Stanley was in receivership and the company never really recovered, the last Stanley steamer being built in 1927.

declined. In 1917, the brothers retired from active involvement with the company. By 1920, Stanley cars had a flat radiator with a dummy filler cap and looked much like any other automobile, but this wasn't enough to overcome the basic problems associated with steam propulsion. When Stanley went into receivership in 1923, it was offering a range of six Series 740 models including tourers, sedans, a roadster and a brougham. Based on a 130 inch wheelbase chassis, all were powered by a 20 horsepower two cylinder engine.

The Steam Vehicle Corporation of America bought the factory and assets for $572,200 in 1924, continuing production at the Newton, Massachusetts, plant until 1927. Thereafter, the Stanley name and its steam-powered automobiles were consigned to history.

Although steam cars would survive into the Thirties, 1923 effectively marked the end of the golden age for this type of automobile. The year also saw the untimely death of president Warren Harding in San Francisco in August; vice president Calvin Coolidge took over in The White House.

Above: The Chevrolet "Copper-Cooled" model was an attempt to produce an air-cooled car using copper fins on the cast iron cylinder block. The subject of several years of experimentation directed by Charles Kettering, when it finally went into production after much delay in 1923, further problems caused the project to be canceled after 759 cars had been built. Only about 100 were actually sold to the public, these were recalled and all but two examples destroyed. The louvers in the radiator grille distinguish the Copper-Cooled Chevy coupe from the standard Series B Superior model.

1924

Walter Percy Chrysler proved to be a man with an outstanding talent for the business of manufacturing automobiles. With an engineering background in the railroad industry, his first connection with cars was as works manager for Buick in 1910. By 1919, the frustrations of working with the volatile Billy Durant proved too much and Chrysler abruptly left the Flint, Michigan, factory, settling on a $10

million pay-off for his stock. Chrysler's next task was to try to sort out the troubled Willys-Overland Company on behalf of the Chase National Bank, for an annual fee of one million dollars. During his two years with Willys, Chrysler became convinced that a six cylinder engine being developed at the Elizabeth, New Jersey, plant by three former Studebaker engineers – Carl Breer, Owen Skelton and Fred Zeder – showed some definite promise.

1921 saw Chrysler at Maxwell, which had merged with Chalmers and was facing difficulties. After the New Jersey Willys factory and six cylinder prototype were bought by Durant, Chrysler took the opportunity to acquire the services of Zeder, Skelton and

Below & left: The styling of the first Chryslers was hardly inspired, but their performance made up for it. The 201.5 cu.in. six cylinder engine produced 68hp thanks to a higher 4.7:1 compression ratio, giving a 70mph top speed, unheard of in such a car.

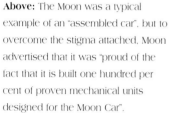

Above: The Moon was a typical example of an "assembled car", but to overcome the stigma attached, Moon advertised that it was "proud of the fact that it is built one hundred per cent of proven mechanical units designed for the Moon Car".

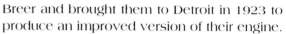

Above: The Doble Series E (shown with a later body by Murphy) was the ultimate steam-powered performance and luxury car ever built and was priced accordingly. Abner Doble was beset by lawsuits in 1924 and fewer than fifty were ever built.

Breer and brought them to Detroit in 1923 to produce an improved version of their engine.

The resulting powerplant provided Walter P. Chrysler with the immediate success of a car bearing his name, replacing the Maxwell. Displacing 201.5 cu.in. the L-head six produced 68bhp at 3200rpm thanks to a higher than average compression ratio of 4.7:1 with a Ricardo type cylinder head, giving the new Chrysler a comfortable top speed of 70mph. Performance of this calibre in a car costing only $1,395 was a major breakthrough and the Chrysler got an enthusiastic reception with 32,000 cars sold in 1924 – a record for first year sales by a new nameplate.

Competition success followed the car's launch, with Ralph Da Palma winning the Mount Wilson hill climb and setting a record two minutes quicker than the previous best by a stock car. Later that year, the same car and driver would cover 1,000 miles on a board track in California, establishing even more performance records. Yet the Chrysler was not just about speed. It had hydraulic brakes on all four wheels, air cleaner, oil filter, a tubular front axle and several other features not normally found on mass-produced, medium priced automobiles. If the engineering of the Chrysler was both excellent and innovative, the same cannot be said of the body styling which was conventional and devoid of any imaginative flair. For years to come, the Chrysler's sound engineering practice would dominate the aesthetic design.

Outwardly, the only hint of speed on the '24 Chrysler was the winged radiator cap, but it was enough to mark the beginning of a major force in the auto industry for the rest of the century. Less of a long term force was Calvin Coolidge who won the presidential election in 1924 using the slogan "Keep Cool With Coolidge" to emphasize his laid back attitude. Also keeping his cool was Clarence Birdseye who introduced frozen food to the world and thereby established another enduring household name.

1925

Herbert H. Franklin was a foundry operator in Syracuse, New York, when, in 1901, he was introduced to a young graduate engineer named John Wilkinson. Upset because he had not been paid for building two prototype air-cooled cars for the New York Automobile Company, Wilkinson took Franklin for a ride in one of them which convinced the foundry owner to enter the automobile industry.

The first of a dozen Franklin automobiles produced in the initial twelve months was delivered in July 1902 and, from then on, the company prospered and grew. Development and improvement of the air-cooled engines continued over the years and subsequently many endurance tests were carried out to prove the superiority of the Franklin over a standard water-cooled car. One such arduous undertaking happened in August 1915 with an 860 mile drive in bottom gear between Walla Walla in Washington and San Francisco. High and second gears were removed from the transmission and the unit sealed before the start, and the engine was never stopped during the running time of 83 hours and 40 minutes – representing an average speed of over 10 miles per hour through some of the most testing terrain.

Up until 1923, the front of a Franklin was readily distinguishable from most other makes of automobile because it didn't have a radiator. Being air-cooled, it obviously didn't need one, and the engine cover was a single cowl, hinged at the front and easily removed for maintenance work. In some respects it bore a passing resemblance to the electric and steam-powered cars of the day. However, in the summer of 1923, a group of Franklin dealers visited the Syracuse factory and threatened to give up their franchises unless the company produced a more conventional-looking car with a dummy radiator grille.

Herbert Franklin was quickly convinced that the dealers were right, but John Wilkinson couldn't accept the idea of a false radiator and resigned in protest. After consultations with both the Walter M. Murphy company in California and J. Frank de Causse in New York, the task of creating a new body design was given to de Causse, and the new Series 11 cars were

Right: Pete DePaolo won the 13th running of the Indy 500 in his Duesenberg at 101.13mph average speed. 1925 was the first year that 110mph was beaten in qualifying.

Below: The Franklin Series 11 with a false radiator was designed by J. Frank de Causse at the insistence of dealers who wanted a conventional-looking car to sell. As well as unusual air-cooled engines, Franklins also used a wooden chassis and full-elliptic suspension.

introduced in March 1925. In addition to the sedans that Franklin were best known for, de Causse's designs included a boat tail speedster – a stylish departure from any of their previous models.

The construction of the Franklin engine bears some investigation. Without the shrouding to direct the air flow, the engine looks rather like a giant, old-fashioned motorcycle unit with six cylinders. Each cylinder is a separate item with the head and barrel cast as one and copper cooling fins attached to the outside. The cooling fan is driven directly off the front of the crankshaft and the air is fed directly to the top of the engine and forced down between the cylinders.

And if the Franklin engine sounds a bit oddball, the rest of the car has its share of quirks too. All Franklins used a wooden chassis exclusively up until 1927, long after other manufacturers had switched to steel frames. The suspension system was also rather special in that it retained the full elliptic leaf springs front and rear, but the cars were noted for an exceptionally comfortable ride.

The restyled 1925 Franklins were a great success and the company continued producing air-cooled automobiles in quantities. It was only a disastrous attempt at an inappropriate V12 luxury car following on from the effects of the Wall Street Crash that caused Franklin to cease trading in 1934.

Quotable quotes of '25 include Calvin Coolidge saying: "The business of America is business", Henry Ford's "Machinery is the modern messiah", but probably the most telling was a judge who declared that the automobile was "a house of prostitution on wheels". John Wilkinson might well have agreed that the Franklin had prostituted its looks by adopting a false radiator, but even in his deepest disgust he would surely never have equated such a fine automobile to a whorehouse.

23

1926

Before there was the Pontiac, there was the Oakland, and before that there was the Pontiac Buggy Company based in the town of Pontiac in Oakland Country, Michigan. The first Oakland came out in 1908, and by the following year the company had been swallowed up by General Motors as part of Billy Durant's expansionist schemes.

Oakland continued to prosper under GM until 1920, when a combination of the recession and poor quality severely affected sales. When Alfred P. Sloan took control of General Motors and started sorting out the mess left behind by Durant, Oakland was an obvious target for improvement. However, Sloan was also concerned that there were a couple of gaps in the rationalized GM range, in particular between Chevrolet and Oldsmobile at the lower end of the price range.

Right: The Chandler Six leads up Lombard Street in San Francisco, "the world's crookedest street". By '26 Chandler were not doing well, and in 1928 they were bought out by Hupp Motor Car Corporation who promptly discontinued the Chandler automobile.

Below: The Pontiac 2-door Coach was fairly unremarkable in concept, but the new marque's models were competitively priced and soon took a big share of the market.

feed lubrication system that produced 40bhp at 2400rpm. The only other problem was the body, and Fisher Body did the tooling at a cut price to have a different design to the Chevy, but it turned out looking much the same.

When announced, the Pontiac came in two closed body styles only – a coupe and a 2-door sedan – which were, according to an Oakland spokesman, "Designed specifically to dominate the field of low-priced sixes". Only the Essex was cheaper in its class, and at $825, 76,742 Pontiacs had been built by the end of 1926.

For the time and price, it had many standard fitments such as exterior sun visor, variable speed windshield wiper, and a roll-down shade for the rear window. The Fisher VV windshield, ("vision and ventilation"), allowed the driver to let fresh air in at two levels.

Later in '26, there were two DeLuxe models which offered one item of particular interest: a foot-controlled head light dimmer switch, an industry first which later became standard.

Only the engine was made by Oakland, the rest was Chevrolet although much was of a tougher specification. The chassis, for example, used heavier gauge steel than the Chevy. The Pontiac could be said to be a beefed-up Chevy with a six cylinder engine using many GM corporate parts – which was just about what Sloan intended. It began inter-changeable manufacture that is still used today.

Although Oakland models continued, the new marque quickly overshadowed its parent and the Oakland name was dropped in 1932. Elsewhere in the industry, Henry Ford was making headlines by paying his workers $6 a day, and US government figures showed that one in six Americans owned a car. In future, quite a few more would buy a Pontiac.

Below: Route 66 was incorporated on November 11th 1926, but there were only 800 miles of paved road between Chicago and Los Angeles at that time. It would carry millions of travelers heading west for a better life and become part of American folklore.

Below right: The Cadillac Series 314 4-door Phaeton featured the "New ninety degree Cadillac" 314.5 cu.in. V8 engine. According to adverts this "makes the Cadillac one of the fastest and most powerful of motor cars".

Sloan proposed a new model to bridge the gap, but rather than create something new, he wanted to use a Chevrolet chassis with a six cylinder engine as the basis for corporate interchangeability. Work alternated between Oakland and Oldsmobile until Alfred R. Glancy took over as general manager of Oakland in 1925. Glancy brought ex-Cadillac man, Ben Anibal, as chief engineer together with Roy Milner as body engineer and Fenn Holden as chassis engineer plus Hermann Schwarze, who had helped Charles Kettering invent the self-starter.

Things proceeded rapidly and the team developed a new six cylinder engine, having decided that the proposed 110 inch wheelbase chassis was basically sound. They proposed a short stroke, 186.5 cu.in. L-head with a three main bearing crankshaft and force-

HISTORIC
CALIFORNIA
US 66
ROUTE

TOW AWAY
NO PARKING
COMMERCIAL VEHICLES
OVER 80 INCHES WIDE
OR 10,000 G.V.W.
UPON ANY STREET FOR
OVER 2 HOURS EXCEPT
LOADING OR UNLOADING
D.M.C. SEC. 11.12.030   SHERIFF 448-9861

1927

Another of Alfred P. Sloan's building blocks in his programme to have General Motors offering a complete range of cars arrived in 1927. The LaSalle filled the gap between the top-priced Buick 6 and the cheapest Cadillac (a difference of $1700 existed between them). It was named after a French explorer who traveled the length of the Mississippi River in 1682. The LaSalle was also to be built as a junior to the Cadillac, another marque named after a French explorer who, in 1701, established a fort that became the city of Detroit.

But it is neither the French connection nor the fact that it was a failure that makes the car significant. What the LaSalle did was to bring stylist Harley Earl to Detroit and establish the practice of first designing a car to look good, then making the engineering fit. Previously, engineering had been dominant and the body-work was a secondary consideration, often produced by an outside supplier. Harley Earl and the LaSalle changed that attitude forever.

Lawrence P. Fisher was general manager of Cadillac and had met Earl at a Cadillac dealership in Los Angeles where Earl was in charge of the custom body shop, producing special cars for celebrities. Fisher asked the young stylist to submit design proposals. As a result, Earl came to Detroit early in 1926 as a consultant under a special contract.

Fisher outlined the project as being "that of designing a quality car of the same family as Cadillac but somewhat lower priced...a production automobile that was as beautiful as the custom cars of the period".

Nowadays, it is hard to see how revolutionary the LaSalle was when it was launched in March 1927. Compared to other GM cars, the LaSalle was lower and longer, with deep-drawn Flying Wing fenders, better proportioned side windows and a new style of body moldings. It was a more integrated design, with few sharp corners and lines that flowed. The LaSalle was a huge sensation when it was seen for the first time by the public.

Sloan was so impressed that he decided to employ Earl on the other GM models. In June, Earl headed a new department, called the Art and Color Section, to direct general body design and conduct research into special car designs. Fifty people made up the department at the start, ten of them designers, but it soon grew into a huge concern with hundreds of employees and established styling as an essential part of the business.

Harley Earl had taken inspiration from the Hispano-Suiza, but the LaSalle was a car in its own right, even though it was promoted as a "Companion Car to Cadillac". It offered Cadillac qualities in a smaller package at a lower price and, with a splendid 303 cu.in. V8 engine, it could perform too. In a test at GM, a LaSalle roadster ran ten hours at an average 95.2mph – almost as fast as that year's Indy 500 winner!

It was a year of sensational happenings –

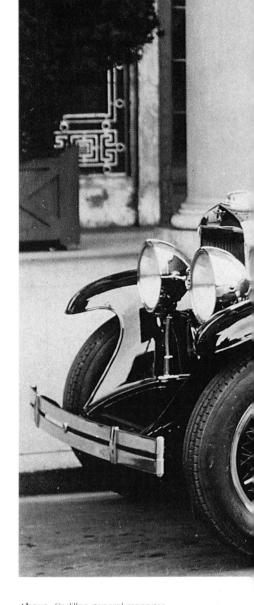

Lindbergh flew solo across the Atlantic, talking pictures arrived with Al Jolson in The Jazz Singer and Babe Ruth hit three home runs as the New York Yankees won the World Series. Against those events, the LaSalle must have seemed small potatoes but it was the starting point of an amazing age in automotive history.

Left: The venerable Ford Model T came to the end of the road in May 1927 when the assembly lines were closed down after more than 15,000,000 Tin Lizzies had been produced. Buyers now wanted something more sophisticated than the old-fashioned (although slightly updated) Model T could offer – even at a bargain basement price.

1928

When the Hudson Motor Car Company were looking to name their cheaper range of four cylinder models planned for a 1919 launch, a map of England was used to find a name with a more up-market appeal. It seemed a strange notion as the car bearing the new badge was to be aimed at the low-buck Model T end of the market, but they finally settled on "Essex" – a county to the east of London. The Hudson people could have also saved themselves the bother of finding a map when you consider that there are towns and counties called Essex in the states of New Jersey, Vermont, Massachusetts and Delaware among others. The choice is even more surprising when you consider that at least three other auto manufacturers called Essex had been launched in the USA.

Whatever the reasons, Essex it was, and although less than a hundred cars were produced in 1918, production leapt the following year and almost 22,000 cars were delivered to the dealers. The most notable thing about Essex in the Twenties was the pricing of its closed models. In an age when open-top cars were generally more popular, and consequently cheaper, Essex made its name producing closed coachwork models for a fraction of the price charged by other manufacturers.

At $1,495, the 1922 Essex four-passenger coach model was the cheapest closed car in America, generating headlines like: "Only $300 More Than Touring Model" in publications such as Motor Age. By 1925, the Essex coach cost five dollars less than the company's open tourer, although prices did equalize later.

Derided as a "packing crate" by the opposition, the Essex coach nevertheless showed the way forward, but the illusion that it was a car produced by a company separate from Hudson gradually diminished. The exemplary F-head 180 cu.in. four was replaced by an L-head 144 cu.in. six cylinder engine during 1924, and performance suffered as a result.

For 1928, Essex enjoyed its best ever sales year, shipping almost 230,000 cars to dealers. Described in some quarters as "low hung", the Essex styling closely resembled the Hudson, but on a slightly smaller scale, with a narrower radiator and a winged mascot replacing the old-fashioned motormeter. Other new styling features included wider fenders and cowl-mounted side lights, plus a

Right: Walter P. Chrysler's 1928 entry into the family car market was the four cylinder Plymouth. Despite four-wheel hydraulic brakes, full pressure engine lubrication, aluminum alloy pistons and a separate hand brake, its first year sales of 50,000 were well below Ford and Chevrolet numbers. However, the timing was impeccable and the Plymouth marque would ensure Chrysler's survival in the economic depression that was to follow.

shorter windshield visor on closed models. A major technical advance was the use of Bendix mechanical brakes on all four wheels.

Essex was leader of the trend which saw 88.5% of cars sold in the USA in 1928 being closed models, whereas less than a decade earlier almost 90% had been open-top – a complete reversal of public taste. While rivals like Chevrolet and Ford were still asking at least $100 more for closed models in '28, the Essex management saw that the future lay in producing enclosed cars as opposed to roadsters and phaetons.

However, the biggest news in the industry that year was the replacement for the Model T Ford. After a shaky start, the Model A went on to become another success. Meanwhile, the stock market boomed, Mickey Mouse made his debut in "Steamboat Willie" – the first cartoon with sound, and Amelia Earhart became the first woman to fly across the Atlantic. It seemed like everything was new in '28.

Above: It is almost impossible to believe today but, in 1927, Ford closed its production lines for six months in order to introduce the Model A in early '28. What is equally unbelievable is that both dealers and customers were willing to wait for such a long time without defecting to other makes, such was the influence wielded by Henry Ford. Although a major advance on the ancient Tin Lizzie, the Model A was completely conventional, powered by a 200 cu.in. L-head four cylinder engine, and nearly five million would be built in four years.

Left: The 1928 Essex Super Six Phaeton is unusual because the Hudson nameplate was leading the revolution towards closed models in the late Twenties. Using a 153 cu.in. six cylinder engine like the rest of the '28 Essex models, Phaeton carried a factory price of $750 – fifteen dollars more than the 2-door sedan – but formed part of the best calendar sales year in company history with 229,887 units produced.

1929

It was the year of Chicago's St. Valentine's Day Massacre and the Wall Street Crash. But while rival gangs of hoodlums were bumping each other off in the Windy City, and ruined stockbrokers were hurling themselves to oblivion from the upper floors of New York's skyscrapers, in Indiana the Cord Corporation were putting the wraps on a new automobile with novel features and great styling that, in many eyes, would make it the most beautiful car of the period. That car was the Cord L-29.

Errett Lobban Cord was a colorful character, a wheeler dealer who, at the beginning of the Twenties, was a successful used-car salesman. By the middle of the decade, however, he had become president and major stockholder of Auburn. Shortly after, he acquired Duesenberg, and by the early Thirties he also

had interests in the Lycoming engine plant, American Airlines, the airplane manufacturer Stinson, and various other businesses in the automotive industry. Cord was an empire builder, but the methods he used to gain controlling interests in companies were dubious.

By 1929, Cord perceived the need for a car that would fill the gap between the attractively-priced Auburn and the mighty Model J Duesenberg, which had recently been introduced by the Cord Corporation. The result was a car that bore his own name: the Cord L-29.

One of the most significant aspects of the L-29 was its front-wheel-drive layout, which had a dramatic effect on the overall styling of the car and made a major contribution to its rakish good looks. The L-29 was not the first American automobile to utilize front-wheel-drive, as for a short period prior to WW1, the Christie had been available with just such an arrangement. Although that project did not succeed, by the late Twenties interest in front-wheel-drive had been revived again following the successful showing of several similarly-equipped race cars in the Indianapolis 500.

Right: The front-wheel-drive layout of the Cord L-29 was based on Harry Miller's 1927 Indy race car, with the final drive and transmission ahead of the engine. The latter was a Lycoming straight-eight similar to that used by Auburn.

Below: The L-29 was an impressive looking car from any angle, as this cabriolet shows. The final drive fits neatly beneath the Duesenberg-inspired grille and radiator surround.

Below right: The long hood and flowing front fenders, coupled with the car's low overall height made even the sedan a stylish automobile. Sadly, the performance did not match the stunning good looks.

Cord employed race car builder Harry Miller and Detroit engineer Cornelius Van Ranst to design the front-wheel-drive set-up for the L-29. Miller's cars had already proved themselves on the track, while Van Ranst was also a keen exponent of the front-wheel-drive layout. Indianapolis race car driver Leon Duray would also act as an adviser on the project.

The team began with Auburn's 298.6 cu.in. flathead, in-line, eight cylinder engine, which produced 115 horsepower at 3300rpm, basing the driveline layout on Miller's 1927 Indy race car. This meant the final drive and transmission had to be ahead of the engine, which had to be turned around so that the flywheel, clutch and chain drive faced forward. The cylinder head was also modified to place the water outlet at the front. A three-speed, sliding-pinion transmission was fitted between the clutch and final drive, the latter having the drive shaft to each wheel equipped with Cardan constant-velocity joints to allow for suspension movement and steering. Miller also designed an inboard braking system, using Lockheed hydraulic components. The

front suspension comprised quarter-elliptic leaf springs and Houdaille-Hershey shock absorbers, which were also used at the rear with semi-elliptic leaf springs.

The car was based initially on a ladder frame, which was common practice at the time. However, when Cord himself drove the prototype over a patch of rough ground, the chassis flexed so much that it caused all the doors of the car to spring open. He immediately ordered Auburn's chief engineer, Herb Snow, to fix the problem, which he did by designing the industry's first X-frame chassis. This provided a much more rigid foundation for the car, and would be copied by other manufacturers as time went on.

Placing the transmission and final drive ahead of the long, straight-eight engine made for a long wheelbase, 137$\frac{1}{2}$ inches in fact. This was much longer than any comparable automobile of the period, but it did have an advantage when it came to designing the bodywork. The Duesenberg-type grille, long sweeping hood and flowing fenders produced a rakish appearance, which was accentuated by the low overall height of the car. Because of the front-wheel-drive layout, no central transmission tunnel was needed in the floor which not only improved foot room for passengers, but also allowed the floor to be a low, step-down design. This ensured that the car retained good headroom for passengers inside while maintaining a relatively low overall height (61 inches for closed cars and 58 inches for open models – most other cars of the period were at least 70 inches high). At the same time, a generous ground clearance of 8 1/2 inches was also possible.

Not only was the Cord L-29 a good looking car, but it was also well appointed inside. The luxurious interiors of closed cars were trimmed in good-quality broadcloth, while open cars received leather upholstery. In both cases, this was set off by silver-plated interior fittings. In addition, the front seats and steering column were adjustable, while fingertip gear shifting was provided by a small lever on the dashboard.

Above: Lincolns for 1929 received a taller and narrower radiator surround, while the previous leather windshield visor was replaced by a tinted glass unit. This is a two-window town sedan, reportedly owned by John Wayne.

Below: While the Whippet made a major contribution to Willys-Overland sales in 1929, it was another casualty of the Wall Street Crash and the Depression. Production ended in 1931.

attempt to overcome the poor sales of 1929, the price was dropped by $800 for 1931, but this did not achieve the desired results. Production was halted at the end of the year, the last 157 cars being built as 1932 models. These had a more powerful 132 horsepower, 322 cu.in. straight-eight engine. This engine had originally been intended to power a new Cord, the L-30, but with the economic situation so poor, and so few L-29s having been built (around 5,000), it was never put into production. Indeed, there would not be another Cord for four years, and in the meantime E. L. Cord would concentrate on his other business interests. Even the new car would only last for two short years, after which Cord sold his empire for a reported $4,000,000, killing off Auburn and Duesenberg in the process.

Below: Chevrolet's Model AC, while similar in appearance to the 1928 Model AB, had an all-new ohv six cylinder engine. The basic design of this engine remained until 1953.

Cabriolet, sedan, brougham and phaeton body styles were available, although many private coachbuilders, on both sides of the Atlantic, used the Cord as the basis for special bodywork. However, beautiful as the cars undoubtedly were, in performance terms they were somewhat sluggish. It took over 30 seconds for the L-29 to reach 60mph from a standing start, while top speed was not much more than 75mph. When compared to contemporary Cadillacs, Lincolns and Packards, the car was definitely a follower rather than a leader, but it did so in such great style.

Although, in theory, the front-wheel-drive layout should have ensured good traction on poor surfaces, in fact much of the weight of the L-29 was over the undriven rear wheels. As a result, the cars gained a poor reputation for dealing with loose surfaces. Furthermore, the constant-velocity joints were lacking in durability, and frequent replacement was necessary.

Although many of the problems that beset the car could have been solved with more development work, Cord himself was impatient to put the L-29 into production and insisted that it be introduced before 1930.

Unfortunately, teething troubles were not the only problems that would affect the sales of the L-29. Two months after the car was introduced in 1929, the stock market on Wall Street crashed, destroying the L-29's chances of becoming a commercial success. In an

34

THE SATURDAY EVENING POST

January 19, 1929

FISHER

The Outstanding Chevrolet
of Chevrolet History
— *a Six in the price range of the four!*

1930

By just about any standards, the outlook in 1930 was bleak for the manufacturers of prestige automobiles. After the stock market collapse, demand for luxury cars had evaporated and many fine marques disappeared. Even though more people held on to their assets during the Depression than is usually suggested, it wouldn't have been acceptable to flaunt good fortune by driving around in a fancy car. So, of those that could actually afford to spend upwards of five thousand dollars on a car, few were willing to take the risk.

Into this atmosphere, came the most fabulous Cadillacs of all time – the Series 452 V16 range. It had a masterpiece of engineering, a 452 cu.in. sixteen cylinder overhead valve unit developing 165bhp and 320 foot pounds of torque. Arranged in a narrow Vee of 45°, with cast iron blocks attached to an aluminum alloy crankcase, the engine was the creation of Cadillac engineer Owen Nacker, and featured a unique system of hydraulically rotated eccentric bushings in the rocker arms to help silence the valve train mechanism.

No expense was spared to make it look impressive and the V16 engine bay was treated to extra plating and polishing. An uncluttered look was achieved by hiding the wiring and plumbing where possible. With smooth power rather than brute acceleration, Cadillac described the performance as "flexible and instantly responsive". Top speed was 90mph, and cruising at 70mph could be enjoyed at length, although a return of eight miles to the gallon may have been hard to tolerate in 1930 – even if gas was only 15 cents a gallon.

The car was built to majestic proportions, based on an enormous 148 inch wheelbase chassis (8 inches longer than the standard V8 models), and there were more than fifty body styles to chose from. Most of the V16 bodies were built to order by Fleetwood following the designs of Harley Earl, and advertised by Cadillac as "Catalog Customs" but there were full custom models that came from the other famous coachbuilders of the day, and even a few bodies from GM's volume supplier Fisher. With such a plethora of styles and sources, it is no wonder that keeping track of all the variations that were constructed has proved to be a difficult task. One style name that frequently crops up in reference books is the

Above: One of the V16 Cadillac models in 1930, the Fleetwood two-door convertible coupe had 19 inch wire wheels with specially balanced whitewall tires, dual sidemounts, twin spot lamps and a huge rear trunk.

Below: Following the success of Oakland with the Pontiac and Cadillac's introduction of the LaSalle, Buick brought out a smaller companion car in 1930 and called it the Marquette. Powered by a 213 cu.in. six cylinder L-head engine, sales of 35,000 were deemed insufficient to keep the Marquette alive and the name was dropped after only one year.

Below: Riding on an enormous 148 inch wheelbase, V16 Cadillacs like this Limousine Brougham weighed over 6,000 pounds. Prices started at $5,350 and went up to $10,000 and beyond for the full custom creations.

"Madame X" – but opinions differ as to exactly what features this model had.

Even those buyers who ordered from the standard Fleetwood range could opt for their own modifications, and the degree of personalization probably means that every one of the three thousand or so V16 Cadillacs sold in 1930 was unique. One only has to look at the eight choices of windshield design that were available – flat vertical, sloping at five different angles, and the vertical Vee – with swing-out or crank-up options, to appreciate the selection facing the well-heeled buyer.

Had Cadillac been an independent company, and not insulated from the economy by General Motors, it is hard to believe it wouldn't have suffered the same fate as all the other manufacturers who were producing luxurious automobiles in small quantities. The V16 wouldn't survive very long, but it set a new standard of excellence that few would equal. That would matter little to the millions of unemployed who were hoping that president Herbert Hoover's measures of tariff controls, emergency job and relief programmes would restore the situation, but things were destined to get worse before they got better.

1931

Marmon not only suffered from being second to Cadillac when introducing a V16 engine, it also had to do without the protection of being part of General Motors. These disadvantages proved impossible to overcome and the Marmon Motor Car Company, of Indianapolis, Indiana, would go into receivership in May 1933, ending a history of building fine automobiles that went back to 1902.

The brainchild of Howard C. Marmon, a brilliant engineer, the Marmon Sixteen (it was never called a V16 by the company) was destined to be the final chapter of a marque story that was nearly all about high performance automobiles. Indeed, what must rank as the most famous racing car of them all, the one that Ray Harroun drove to victory in the first Indy 500 in 1911, is the Marmon Wasp. Apart from being based in Indianapolis, Marmon's connection with the speedway remained until the end: every Sixteen came with a guarantee that the car had completed two laps of the Indy track at over 100mph.

Acceleration was brisk too, Marmon boasting that it would go from five to sixty miles an hour in 20 seconds, a feat few others could match. And, long before drag racing became a recognized sport, Marmon literature for the Sixteen proclaimed: "When the light turns green it leaves its neighbor far behind". The reasons for the superior performance came from extensive use of aluminum alloy in the 490 cu.in. 200 horsepower V16 engine which had a 6:1 compression ratio – the highest in the industry at the time. Although of a similar 45° narrow Vee configuration to the Cadillac motor, the Marmon unit weighed around 370 pounds less, giving a much better power to weight ratio. Lightweight construction was also a feature of the car as a whole, with hood and splash aprons, head light and tail lamp brackets, all made of aluminum.

Bodies were designed by Walter Dorwin Teague, built by LeBaron, and represented as big a departure from previous Marmons as did the V16 from the eight and six cylinder units seen in other company models. From the sloping V-shaped radiator grille to the low roof line, it represented a totally new concept

Below: The magnificent Marmon Sixteen performed with exhilaration that matched its looks, thanks to a 490 cu.in. V16 engine and lightweight construction. Sadly, it arrived at a time when the demand for luxury cars had evaporated, and the Marmon company would become extinct as a result.

Above: "Smoothness of a Six and the Economy of a Four" was what the Plymouth PA promised, thanks to new Floating Power rubber engine mounts which reduced vibration. After a $2.5 million development by Chrysler, it moved the marque into third place behind Ford and Chevrolet.

Above: By 1931, LaSalle was using the same 353 cu.in. V8 L-head engine as its Cadillac parent and was becoming more like Cadillac in other ways too – and suffering from the confusion of identity. A decline in yearly sales to 10,000 units didn't help future prospects much either.

for Marmon. But timing was its downfall. Not only did Marmon launch it at the beginning of the depression, bad enough timing in itself, but following the display of the Sixteen at auto shows during the winter of 1930/31 it was April before the first car was delivered. The delay put Marmon even further behind Cadillac who were themselves struggling to sell their V16 in any significant numbers.

Pricing was another problem. While the Sixteen wasn't cheap, it undercut the Cadillac V16, and many believe that Marmon couldn't have made much profit on the cars they sold. Price cuts in succeeding years only served to make things worse. In the end, less than 400 Sixteens were produced in three years.

Marmon did produce other cars in 1931, and tried to move away from the limited production luxury market after George Williams took over as company president in 1924. The eight cylinder Little Marmon lasted one model year, 1927, and the Roosevelt (another eight cylinder car, this time priced at under $1,000) also failed to last after an initial demand saw production hit 22,300 units in 1929. Williams couldn't have forseen the economic catastrophe coming, and it hit the company hard. By '31, annual output was less than six thousand cars, and the Roosevelt had been dropped as a separate marque though the car itself remained in slightly revised form as the Marmon Model 70.

By 1933, the Sixteen was the only Marmon. Arriving in a year when over 800 banks failed, it's not surprising it was shortlived. It was also the year that Will Rogers said: "We are the first nation to go to the poorhouse in an automobile". The trouble was, not enough chose to go in a Marmon.

1932

If we were to adapt a modern day saying to suit the circumstances of 1932, it might run something along the lines of: "When the going gets tough, Henry Ford gets things going". For, when it came time to making things happen or shaking up an established method of doing a certain task, nobody was as effective as the founder of the Ford Motor Company. It's true to say that he was also cantankerous, irascible, pig-headed, stubborn, and much worse besides on occasions.

It's also true that he had a vast army of men that he could command to do his bidding, and would often set them impossible targets to test out an idea or prove a theory. Further more, history has a way of only telling us of the successes achieved by great

Right: Ford urged dealers to get customers to try out the V8, saying "Driving means buying". The center salesman is in a rare 4-door Phaeton with models to illustrate chassis construction.

Below: By far the most popular of the Model 18s, the V8 powered Tudor sedan sold for $450 in standard form and $500 for the DeLuxe as seen here with pin stripes and cowl lights.

men, and the mistakes they made along the way are often forgotten. There's no doubt Henry Ford made his fair share of errors while amassing a fortune from the Model T, but when old Henry got something right, it was usually a spectacular success.

Just such a brainwave was his decision to put a V8 engine in the 1932 models at the height of the depression when thirteen million people were unemployed, the average wage had dropped by 60% since 1929 and even US President Herbert Hoover and baseball hero Babe Ruth had volunteered to take pay cuts. Henry's reasoning might not have been based on a very logical train of thought – the main purpose being to outdo his arch rivals at Chevrolet. "We're going from a four to an eight, because Chevrolet is going to a six", is what he is quoted as saying in 1929.

But although the idea came about from a fixation with competition, the execution of putting it into production was the stuff from which Ford legends were made. Early in 1932, when the foundry at the huge River Rouge plant was crying out for help to overcome the problems it had in casting the new V8 engine against incredibly short deadlines, it was suggested that extra draughtsmen should be hired to get engineering drawings done. Ford's reply was: "Sorensen can make all you want just from a sketch on the back of an envelope", an attitude brought about by Henry's inability to understand proper drawings and his dislike of them being used. While "Cast Iron Charlie" Sorensen was undoubtedly a wizard when it came to solving the diffi-

culties encountered with manufacturing large quantities of a complex new design, even he couldn't do it all from just a scribble on the back of an envelope. Nevertheless, Sorensen had to agree with his boss at the time, but the necessary blueprints were produced without Henry's knowledge.

Such subterfuge was often employed when Henry Ford was involved in making decisions about how something should be done and as far as the mechanical side of the Model 18 was concerned, Henry was very much in control. An article published in the Detroit News in February 1932 carried this quote from Edsel Ford: "My father is never happier than when he is solving some big mechanical problem. When the Model A was brought out he left many things to others, but I have never seen him give such attention to detail as he is now. He works for hours at a time trying to eliminate a single part. He figures that the fewer the parts in a car, the less the risk of trouble."

But Henry's quest for fewer parts didn't stop him from holding on to old-fashioned ideas, long after they had been discarded by other manufacturers and often in complete contradiction to common sense. Hydraulic brakes were not acceptable, the mechanical rod system giving rise to the Ford slogan "safety of steel from toe to wheel", but hydraulic shock absorbers were deemed to be okay, despite being more expensive. Transverse leaf springs were another thing that Ford would insist upon in the car's suspension design for many years to come.

THE AMERICAN AUTOMOBILE

Fortunately, thanks to his preoccupation with the nuts and bolts of his cars, Henry left styling matters to his son Edsel, saying "He knows style – how a car should look". Edsel was assisted by Joe Galamb and Eugene T. "Bob" Gregorie and although it has been suggested that LeBaron or body manufacturers Briggs also had a hand in the design, this seems unlikely apart from the usual small modifications that might be requested by any supplier to make a component easier to produce. When compared to its predecessor the Model A, the Model 18 (the Model B shared the identical bodyshell but used a four cylinder engine) featured a more rounded look, especially on the radiator grille, front fenders and roof leading edge – not streamlining but a

definite move in that direction, away from the utilitarian school of thought.

After some of the most intensive development work ever seen in peacetime, the first of the new Ford V8 engines came off the line in March 1932 and was ceremonially stamped by Henry Ford with the numbers 18-1, representing the first eight cylinder and the first of its type. Displacing 221 cu.in. and rated at 65bhp, it was the first such engine in volume mass production. Despite predictions, initial V8 production was slow, with many rejects. Once the cars finally got into the hands of the eager customers (cars ordered at the launch in early April weren't delivered until August in most cases), it was found that the new engine suffered many shortcomings. Overheating, excessive oil consumption, bearings and pistons wearing out rapidly, blocks cracking, fuel pump problems and much else besides, brought in numerous complaints and the Ford Motor Company was forced to issue corrective remedies and free replacement parts which cost millions of dollars.

In an attempt to counter some of this negative feedback, Ford staged a test to demonstrate the durability and reliability of the V8. A car was driven night and day around a 32 mile course in the Mojave Desert, California, for 33 days. At the end of the test, the car had covered 33,301 miles – equivalent to going one and a third times around the world according to the Ford publicists – at an average speed of 41.8mph (including stops), achieved 19.64 miles per gallon and used "only" 1.5 pints of oil for every thousand miles.

Whether this exercise had the required effect is difficult to judge, and in more recent times it is the recommendations that Ford received from notorious gangsters like John Dillinger and Clyde Barrow (of Bonnie and Clyde fame) for the V8's superior performance in getaways that have often been given greater prominence. That the Ford could provide previously unknown speed and acceleration in a low-priced car when its engine was running on song is undeniable, but the haste to produce it caused no end of problems – some of which took years to eradicate.

If engineering was causing Ford plenty of headaches, things were also far from tranquil on other fronts. Four demonstrators were killed during the Ford Hunger March to the Rouge plant on 6th March, organized to protest at the lack of jobs – after being idle for months while the new car was being prepared, workers discovered that there were less than half the jobs on offer than before. And to cap it all, much to Henry's chagrin, Chevrolet still outsold Ford by a wide margin as the Dearborn company had its lowest calendar year production since 1914 and lost $75 million in the process. The V8 would go on to be a winner and the 1932 Ford would become an automotive icon, but few in those dark days could have guessed it.

1933

Most truly great automobiles have an exclusive styling feature that makes them instantly identifiable. For Pierce-Arrow, it was having the head lamps incorporated into the fenders. Designed at the Buffalo, New York, factory by Herbert Dawley and patented in 1913, ordinary head lights were an option until 1932, yet without head lamps on the fender, it just wasn't a Pierce-Arrow.

Famed for producing cars in the luxury car market, by 1915 Pierce-Arrow could count 12,000 automobiles that had found satisfied wealthy customers since the company's start in 1901. But, in the following years, things weren't to run nearly as smoothly as the silky six cylinder engines used in their cars. In fact, their insistence on staying with the six was the start of their problems, as most other prestige makers soon offered eights, or even twelves, and Pierce-Arrow subsequently fell behind; it took until 1920 for Pierce-Arrow to shift the steering wheel from the right-hand side to the left to conform with the standard used by the rest of the industry for years.

In the early Twenties, a merry-go-round of management changes exacerbated the situation and, by 1926, Pierce-Arrow was in trouble. By 1928 company president, Myron Forbes, could see that Pierce-Arrow needed help and negotiated a merger with Studebaker. Things perked up considerably and in 1929 came a new eight cylinder engine. Sales doubled to 10,000 units that year, but this was not to last.

1933 proved to be the crunch year, although it might not have seemed so at the outset. First there was the superb V12 engine. Designed by Karl Wise and introduced in '31, it was equal to any other twelve cylinder powerplant, with seven main bearings instead of four as used by Packard and Cadillac. Then there was the pioneering use of hydraulic tappets – another first for Pierce-Arrow, ranking alongside its power braking system for technical innovation. Sales increased in early '33, but a crippling strike by tool and die makers interrupted the recovery.

Studebaker protected Pierce from the

Above: The Pierce Silver Arrow was streamline styling at its elegant best. Designed by Philip Wright, the curvaceous sedan was capable of 120mph, but at $10,000, it was one of the most expensive on the market.

Below: The Ford De Luxe Fordor sedan was powered by either a four cylinder engine or a V8. Styled by Edsel Ford, Joe Galamb and Bob Gregorie, the Tudor was the best-selling version at $450.

worst effects of the Depression, but it had over-extended itself and went bankrupt in the spring of '33. Albert E. Erskine, president of Studebaker (and Pierce-Arrow too, following Forbes' resignation in '29) committed suicide in July and, in August, Pierce was sold off to a group of bankers and businessmen.

In the midst of all this upheaval, came Philip Wright's streamlined masterpiece – the Pierce Silver Arrow. Promising "in 1933 the car of 1940", this tapered-tail fastback 4-door sedan caused a sensation when it appeared at the New York Automobile Show. Said to be capable of 120mph, with a cruising speed of

80mph thanks to the 175bhp 462 cu.in. V12 engine, the wind-cheating shape (developed with the aid of a wind tunnel) foretold many future styling features. There were no running boards, the fenders were smoothly integrated into the body and every joint was precise.

Priced at $10,000, the Silver Arrow was the most expensive US car on the market, apart from Duesenberg, and only five were made. Some of the features were incorporated in '34 models, but sales were in decline and, after several more attempts at reorganization, the company finally folded in 1938.

Franklin Delano Roosevelt was inaugurated as the 32nd President of the United States at the start of '33 and set in motion his 100 Days program to boost the economy. Prohibition was abolished, but Pierce-Arrow had little to celebrate as, despite the first small signs of recovery, the days of such an expensive hand-made car were numbered.

Above: The Willys 77 was powered by an ultra-economical 134 cu.in. four cylinder engine that could achieve up to 30 miles per gallon and reach 70mph. Despite a low price of $395, its unusual styling didn't sell, and Willys declared bankruptcy in 1933. The marque would survive after reorganization.

Below: Oldsmobile called its 1933 models the "style leaders" and production more than doubled over the previous bad year. Six and eight cylinder models were offered, with shorter wheelbase sixes in the majority. "No-Draft Ventilation" with pivoting wind wings was developed by Fisher Body and featured on all GM models this year.

1934

For a company whose cars were dominated by engineering considerations, almost to the exclusion of styling innovations, the arrival of the Airflow from Chrysler in January '34 must have been a surprise to many people. But even more of a surprise, perhaps, is that the Airflow indeed came directly from a desire for better automotive engineering rather than a decision to create a design statement.

Unfortunately for Chrysler, the Airflow was proof that while good engineers can be relied on to crack difficult technical problems, even the best of them sometimes fail to appreciate that styling shouldn't be completely ruled by function. The engineer's view of what looks right is usually determined by what works best, not what appeals to the potential customer. Throughout modern history there have been numerous examples of ideas that were too far ahead of popular taste and had to be abandoned as a result – the Chrysler Airflow is just one such mistake.

Inspiration for the wind tunnel research that led to the creation of the Airflow is said to have come to Chrysler engineer Carl Breer

Below: The Chrysler Custom Imperial Airflow 4-door Sedan. Limited production Custom Imperial models were the first to use a curved one-piece windshield in '34 and also had vacuum assisted brakes. Although featuring all the body trim of a 1934 example, the pointed grille is of the type introduced for the '35 model year by stylist Raymond Dietrich in an attempt to revitalize sales from the disastrous slump – it wasn't enough.

back in 1927 when he saw a squadron of air craft flying in formation. It set in motion a train of thought about the lack of aerodynamics involved in the design of car bodies, so he had a small scale wind tunnel constructed where he carried out tests on wooden blocks. The next stage was to have a much larger wind tunnel built at the Chrysler Highland Park research center. One of the most interesting observations arising from the experiments was that most cars produced less wind resistance when placed backwards in the tunnel. In a later interview, Carl Breer said he remembered looking out of his office window at the parking lot and thinking: "Just imagine all those cars running in the wrong direction all this time".

One of the first elements he found to reduce wind resistance was a sloping back and this led to other fundamental design changes. In order to give sufficient headroom for rear seat passengers, they had to be moved forward, which in turn caused the front seat to shift and this had a knock-on effect of pushing the engine out over the front axle – a completely new idea. But important though streamlining had become, there were many other factors that the team of Breer, Owen Skelton, Fred Zeder and Oliver Clark were working on with the new car. Improved ride qualities through better weight distribution, more interior room and greater structural strength were also targets for the engineers.

With a conventional Thirties car, the majority of the weight would be supported by the

rear axle, typically in a ratio of 60:40%. By moving the engine forward, the Airflow now had a much better front to rear balance with 55% at the front and 45% at the rear. It wasn't simply a matter of moving the engine forward, however, it had to be tilted at an angle of 5° to keep the transmission tunnel profile down. This, in turn, required a special oil pan to cope with suspension movement as one third of the block was ahead of the front axle. Longer leaf springs were used to further enhance the ride characteristics and some reports concluded that the Airflow came close to fulfiling the "Floating Power" phrase used in Chrysler advertising. Also, seat width was increased by a whopping ten inches to give unrivaled roominess for six people to travel in comfort.

Structurally too, the Airflow differed considerably from the norm, using an all-steel cage fixed to the chassis rails, rather than the traditional method of wooden reinforcement members for the steel body panels favored by most other manufacturers. The lightweight cage, resembling a modern NASCAR racing stock car safety frame, closely followed the roof and body lines providing a rigid mounting for the panels and was a step along the road towards full unitary construction and the elimination of a separate body and chassis. One other feature of note was the first use of a one-piece curved windshield on the special Custom Imperial limited production models.

But no matter what technical advancements were achieved with the Airflow, it was the body styling that would sell the car to the public. Today we can look at the "waterfall" grille and rounded front end and appreciate what they were doing, but back then it was seen as an ugly beast. That wasn't the case at the New York Automobile Show where the car made its debut, and enough of the more sophisticated metropolitan audience were sufficiently impressed to place orders which added up to several thousand in total. And several high-profile personalities in the fashion and design world expressed enthusiasm for the ultra-modern shape. It was a fairly promising start, but by no means all of the big city observers liked the design, and some warning signs might have been noticed.

The immediate problem faced by Chrysler was fulfiling these initial orders. Getting the radical design into production proved more difficult than had been envisaged and there was a three or four month delay (depending on the model) before deliveries began. This hold-up proved to be critical. In the interim, rival manufacturers were able to circulate negative rumors about the strange-looking Airflow and without any cars in use to counter this propaganda, Chrysler suffered from a loss of consumer confidence in the new automobile. It also has to be admitted that when the first cars were actually delivered there was some shortfall in the build quality, which didn't help at all.

It wasn't just Chrysler that was affected; DeSoto used the Airflow design exclusively for its '35 model range and sales tumbled as a result. The Chrysler marque fared slightly better because of the line of more conventional models with the Airstream name that were produced alongside the Airflow and so

Above: The Brewster nameplate was revived in 1934 by the Springfield Manufacturing Corporation of Springfield, Massachusetts, to produce custom-bodied cars, usually based on a Ford V8 chassis. They featured a sensational heart-shaped grille, split bumpers and flaring fenders. Built to the highest standards, and priced at $3,500, ostentatious Brewster models like this convertible sedan were inappropriate for the time and the company was wound up in 1936 after production of between 100 and 300 cars.

Left: Typical of the conventional style of Chrysler's Dodge and Plymouth divisions in 1934 is this Dodge Senior Six sedan produced for export. It consists of a Plymouth body, chassis and running gear with minor trim alterations to make it look like a Dodge.

46

helped limit losses. In a year when auto industry sales rose by 40% the combined total for Chrysler and DeSoto dropped by almost 10% to about 50,000 units. Of those, only 15,000 were Airflow models – it was a dismal verdict on a technically superior vehicle.

Thankfully for the corporation as a whole, Plymouth and Dodge hadn't used the Airflow shape and their sales remained buoyant. The situation wasn't as disastrous as it might have been for Chrysler, partly due to sales of the standard Airstream models, but also to the fact that the Airflow had been designed to keep tooling and manufacturing costs down.

The Chrysler panic buttons were hit and stylist Raymond Dietrich was hired to rescue the situation. He introduced a grille with a peak to replace the original waterfall design for '35 but sales still declined. Chrysler kept faith with the Airflow until 1937, giving it annual facelifts to try and improve public acceptance but the resistance to the unusual shape just couldn't be overcome and it was dropped.

Setbacks of a more permanent kind were suffered by the criminal fraternity during 1935 as bank robbers Bonnie Parker and Clyde Barrow were killed and became enshrined in folk lore. And Public Enemy Number One – John Dillinger – was killed by the FBI, as were hoodlums Pretty Boy Floyd and Baby Face Nelson. It proves that just like crime, it doesn't always pay to be first in the automotive field with a revolutionary idea, no matter how sound the engineering behind it!

Right: The Packard Eleventh Series for 1934 (the sequence started in 1924 with the First Series) included many magnificent models such as this convertible coupe. Packard sales improved to 8,000 and dealers would often bring cars to prospective customers' homes for test drives as part of the service.

1935

Sometimes the past can come back and hit you in the face, reminding you that it's all been done before. To use an automotive analogy, it's like looking in the rear view mirror and seeing that engraved message warning that "objects may be closer than they seem". Since Chrysler introduced the Plymouth Voyager and Dodge Caravan in 1984, minivans, MPVs or people movers have become some of the biggest selling models of the Nineties and nearly every manufacturer has an example. But look at the Stout Scarab of 1935, read the specification and marvel at how farsighted was its creator William B. Stout.

While the Scarab was influenced by his pioneering work on all-metal aircraft, Stout's background also included automotive jobs. His first taste of car design was in 1913 when he was an editor on Motor Age, but his proposed cyclecar never made it into production due to lack of finance. Stout had better luck with the Imp cyclecar when he was general sales manager for McIntyre, but that was a commercial failure and he moved to Scripps-Booth at the end of 1914 where he was chief engineer. That position was also brief, and in 1916 he joined the aircraft division of Packard.

All his life, Stout was a prolific inventor (he filed more patents than anyone else except Thomas Edison) and he introduced the internally-braced, cantilevered all-metal wing and corrugated aluminum outer skin to American aviation. Stout also had a gift for self-promotion, as shown by a letter he sent to Detroit industrialists, to raise money for a project, which said: "We want to build a metal plane. If you join us it will cost money. One thousand dollars. No more, no less. And for your thousand dollars you will get one definite promise. You will never get your money back."

But it was joining forces with Henry and Edsel Ford that really got things going. The Fords built Stout a new facility in Dearborn, Michigan, and the Stout Metal Airplane Co was established as a division of The Ford Motor Company. The result was the 2-AT, the first all-metal aircraft built in the USA, which had exceptional load carrying capabilities. In 1925, Henry Ford decided to buy out William Stout's share of the company, and he became the head of an independent airline while still developing aircraft. Stout Air Services operated Ford 4-AT Tri-Motor airliners, and was the first airline to offer in-flight meals (sand-

48

Left: Stout Scarab advertising consisted of "A challenge and a prophecy..." but the predictions that the unusual car would be a major influence on automobile design was about half a century out.

Below: The minimum body overhang due to the wheels being positioned at the extremities and the aerodynamic shape were part of futuristic Scarab's unique features, but poor rearward vision was a major handicap.

wiches and coffee) and employ uniformed Flight Escorts. Stout's aircrew also wore the company uniforms of blue trimmed with gold braid, a suggestion by Henry Ford that it would "lend dignity to their profession".

Stout sold his airline to the newly-formed United Airlines and turned his mind to other things. In 1932, he started Stout Engineering Laboratories in Detroit where he built the first Scarab prototype. It wasn't until 1935, however, that he deemed the Scarab was ready for production when he introduced a second, steel-bodied version (the original had a dura-luminum alloy body). Everything about the Scarab was unusual – unit construction and streamlined in shape, it had a rear-mounted 85hp Ford V8 coupled to a transaxle/differential unit modified from a three-speed transmission, plus coil spring suspension all round.

The Scarab interior was equally unorthodox: in a huge 7ft 6ins by 5ft 7ins floor area, only the driver's seat was fixed, the others were loose to enable them to be moved to any position. A folding table was provided for eating or playing cards and there was a rear

davenport seat which converted into a full-length couch. One magazine described the Scarab's cabin thus: "The interior of the car is extremely comfortable and roomy, with a table and movable chairs. It gives passengers the feeling of traveling in a hotel room".

Above: Hudson's '35 sedan models had all-steel roofs but were otherwise the same as '34 models. The main new item was a 93hp, 212 cu.in. six cylinder engine alongside the 254 cu.in. 113 hp straight eight used before.

Whether people would want to travel in such surroundings is another matter, but Stout took the Scarab on trips to promote it and drew large crowds whenever he stopped. A report on a visit to Bartlesville, Oklahoma, describes Stout as "one of the nation's foremost mechanical engineers, responsible for many modern perfections in both aeronautical and automotive design...the Scarab seems destined to mark a new milepost in motor design".

Stout's advertising outlined the advanced features – draftless ventilation with rain, dust and insect filter; thermostatically-controlled heat; electric door locks; insulation against sound and temperature; smooth lines minimizing wind noise – things we now take for granted. Stout made this prediction: "The new Scarab will set all future styles in motor cars. The following features now exclusive to the Scarab, will be adopted by all makers of fine cars within three years. These features mark the final departure of motor car engineering from all horse-and-buggy tradition".

Stout's advertisements for the Scarab issued a bit of a challenge: "Created after a decade of aircraft and automotive research, the Scarab rear-engine motor car comes as a friendly but direct challenge to the necessary conservatism of the big-production motor car manufacturers. The Scarab expresses Vision vs Conservatism; Functional Design vs Traditional Design; Individuality vs Standardization; Fine Craftsmanship vs Mass Production. Produced by a group whose soundness of experience and engineering finesse is thoroughly established, the obvious 'rightness' of the Scarab design is its greatest challenge".

Stout's confidence was misplaced. He priced the Scarab "from five thousand dollars" which placed it in Cadillac territory. And to enhance exclusivity, production was limited to 100 cars in 1936, with demonstration by invitation only! Despite its merits – and there were quite a few – the Scarab's concept and styling proved too advanced for the period. In the end, less than ten were built (sources differ between five and nine) and a couple of those found their way to Hollywood where such an outrageous-looking vehicle would have fitted right in with the movie star set.

These days, the streets and highways are crowded with MPVs and minivans, and while it might have pleased Stout to see his prophecy come true, it would undoubtedly have given him more pleasure had his Scarab been the success he hoped for. As it was, like so many visionaries, Stout's ideas were ahead of their time and his dreams ended in failure.

Failure of a more traumatic nature was facing farmers after years of drought and the southern plains turned into the notorious Dust Bowl as dust clouds darkened the skies. Forced to become migrants, many headed west in their jalopies in search of work. Those who could afford new cars found General Motors switching to all-steel Turret-Top roofs without the customary fabric insert. Other metal tops in the news were on beer cans which appeared for the first time; was it a coincidence that Alcoholics Anonymous was also founded?

Right: Ford's slogan for 1935 was 'Greater Beauty, Greater Comfort, and Greater Safety' and the DeLuxe Phaeton is a good example of the longer, wider and faster automobiles being produced by the company. The year's most popular Ford was the 2-door Tudor sedan which sold over 322,000; the more expensive Phaeton sold only 6,073, but the lack of roll-up windows probably didn't help. Note the front doors are now front-hinged and this was the last year for outside horns and wire wheels.

Left: Oldsmobile added the all-metal 'Turret-Top' roof as part of a complete restyle for 1935 although the car's mechanics stayed much as before. This MGM publicity photo shows movie star Freddie Bartholomew polishing his new Olds 4-door Touring Sedan, a gift from studio head Louis B. Mayer following his success in the leading role in David Copperfield.

1936

In October 1936, the first 300-mile international road race was held at New York's Roosevelt Raceway at Westbury on Long Island. The track had been built on the site of the airfield from which Charles Lindbergh had taken off on his daring solo transatlantic flight in 1927, and the racers were vying for the George Vanderbilt Cup. It was ultimately won by Italian Tazio Nuvolari in a Scuderia Ferrari Alfa Romeo. The highest-placed American finisher, however, was Mauri Rose, who took eighth place in an Offenhauser-powered Miller car.

Rose's placing was not much for American sports fans to cheer about but, earlier in the year, they had good reason to be happy. Black athlete, Jesse Owens, triumphed at the Olympic Games in Berlin, much to the chagrin of Adolf Hitler and his Nazi followers. Their racist doctrine could not contemplate the success of anyone other than a blond, blue-eyed arian and Hitler stormed out rather than present Owens with his gold medal.

It would not be long before the Nazi hordes would be storming through Europe, but such a prospect would be far from the minds of Americans that year. US car buyers, particularly in the luxury market, would be considering the new streamlined Lincoln Zephyr. This radical design employed a novel method of construction and was technically advanced in many ways.

The Zephyr began life outside the Ford Motor Co, being conceived by John Tjaarda, a stylist at Briggs Manufacturing Co. Briggs built bodies for Ford, and the new design was intended as a project to sell to Ford. An early prototype was constructed in 1934, but it was far too radical for production. Although it was powered by a Ford flathead V8, this was mounted in the rear with a swing-axle final drive sprung by a transverse leaf spring. The cost of making this set-up work, plus the likely buyer resistance to such an unusual arrangement, even if it were backed by the Ford name, made the idea a non-starter.

Above: Seen from above, the streamlined shape of the Lincoln Zephyr, with its tapering nose, is quite obvious. Head lights set into the front fenders and full fender skirts at the rear added to its sleek look.

However, the overall streamlined shape of the car appealed to Edsel Ford, who felt that it had possibilities as a front-engined car. Edsel had been responsible for transforming the fortunes of Lincoln during the Twenties and early Thirties. When he took charge of the

Above: The new 267.3 cu.in. flathead V12 engine was similar in design to Ford's V8, but had its cylinders set at a narrower angle. Despite lubrication problems, it performed well giving the Zephyr a top speed of 90mph.

Above: Two body styles were offered in 1936: a 2-door sedan and a 4-door sedan. The teardrop shape was in evidence throughout the car, including the rear lights and fenders.

Right: Buyers had a choice of taupe broadcloth or tan bedford cord upholstery but, if they paid extra, they could have the interior trimmed in leather, as shown here. This 4-door has a glazed divider between front and rear seats.

53

THE AMERICAN AUTOMOBILE

division in 1922, Lincoln had only recently been saved from receivership by his father, Henry Ford, and was building expensive, old-fashioned cars. Under Edsel, the company soon began producing some of the most beautiful automobiles ever created.

Henry Ford believed that a car should be engineered first, with the bodywork designed to suit. But Edsel had other ideas. He placed good styling first and foremost, so much so that he authorized the creation of Ford's first styling department under the direction of Eugene T. Gregory. The latter was now given the task of refining Tjaarda's design to allow for the installation of an engine and radiator at the front of the car.

In the original, rear-engined design, the nose of the car had been very narrow and pointed; Gregory managed to widen this sufficiently to accommodate the engine, radiator and radiator grille, while retaining the sense of a narrow, pointed nose. The result was a beautiful, streamlined body, based on a 122 inch wheelbase, that was quite unique for its day. Much use was made of the teardrop shape, not just in the overall style of the body, but also in individual features, such as tail lights, fender skirts and grille emblem.

The uniqueness of the car's styling was matched by its method of construction. Even in its rear-engined prototype guise at Briggs, the car had featured unibody construction, the body panels being welded together with various strengthening members to produce a strong structure that had no need of a separate chassis. The fabric roof insert, found on all other closed Ford cars at the time, was also disposed of and the Zephyr had a solid steel roof panel in its place.

The narrow tapering nose of the Zephyr needed a small, narrow engine. At the time, all Lincolns were powered by V12 engines, and it was felt that the new car would have to be similarly equipped to be considered a Lincoln. However, the existing powerplant was too large for the sleek design, so Lincoln's chief engineer, Frank Johnson, designed a new engine to suit the car. While this was based on Ford's successful flathead V8, it naturally had four extra cylinders. To achieve the narrow profile, the cylinder banks were angled at 75° (they were set at 90° in the V8). The one-piece, cast-iron block was fitted with aluminum cylinder heads and alloy steel pistons. With a bore and stroke of 2¾ and 3¾ inches respectively, the new V12 displaced 267.3 cu.in. and produced 110 horsepower at 3900rpm.

Backing the engine was a three-speed manual transmission with floorshift. This was connected to a torque-tube drive, which was standard Ford practice.

While the engine and bodywork were completely new, some aspects of the car were definitely behind the times. Not only was the Zephyr equipped with mechanical brakes on all four wheels, but its suspension system was also outdated: transverse leaf springs were fitted at front and rear with solid axles. While the mechanical brakes would be replaced by Bendix hydraulic units in 1939, the transverse springs would soldier on for

Right: Paramount starlet, Gloria Shea, poses for a publicity shot on the front fender of a '36 Chevrolet Master Deluxe sport coupe. The Master series was updated this year with a larger, more rounded grille, while the Standard models took on a similar style. The revisions obviously worked, as Chevrolet gained the number one spot in automobile sales that season.

some time to come. Even the new engine received a lot of criticism, particularly concerning the lubrication system. To ensure that the engine ran reliably, owners were advised to change the oil every 1000 miles. Some engines never made it to the 30,000 mile mark before expiring.

Although sales were slow when the first Zephyrs appeared in November 1935, they soon picked up, and total production for the year came to 15,000 cars, a big improvement on Lincoln's performance for the previous year, which totaled 1,400 cars. No doubt, its revolutionary styling produced some initial resistance, but the Zephyr was well priced, at a fraction of the cost of earlier coach-built models offered by the company.

When the Zephyr went into production, Briggs built most of the car, while Lincoln carried out final assembly work, such as fitting the engine, transmission and suspension along with the hood and fenders, then painting and trimming the cars. However, this arrangement was terminated shortly after the car was introduced. When the Zephyr needed updating for 1937, this was handled by Ford's styling department, who made subtle changes to the design that not only significantly improved the car's appearance, but also kept costs to a minimum by utilizing most of the original tooling.

The Lincoln Zephyr would continue to be updated and restyled until 1949. Throughout, it remained a sleek, streamlined design in keeping with the original.

Above: In 1936, Errett Lobban Cord made a last attempt to move in to the specialty market, with the 810. The new Cord had striking "coffin nose" styling by Gordon Buehrig and the range comprised two sedans, a phaeton and a convertible, all on a 125 inch wheelbase and powered by a 125 horsepower Lycoming V8. The car became the 812 in 1937, with an optional supercharger, but production was halted that year following Cord's departure from the auto industry.

Right: Racers round the first turn during the Vanderbilt Cup 300 mile international road race at Roosevelt Raceway.

1937

Disasters in the air were major news in 1937. After a successful transatlantic crossing, the massive German airship Hindenburg exploded while coming into land on 6th May with great loss of life. Out over the Pacific, pioneer aviatrix, Amelia Earhart, disappeared and no trace of her, her companion or her airplane was ever found. While ostensibly she was on a record-breaking flight, it was rumored that she was working for the government and spying on the Japanese, who shot her down. Whether or not this is true, no one will ever know, but it is far more likely that the weather, machine problems or simply fatigue caused her to crash and be swallowed up in the vastness of the ocean.

In the world of international auto racing, Americans faced a disappointing result in the Vanderbilt Cup at Roosevelt Raceway. The first three machines across the finish line were all from Europe. In the lead was Bernd Rosemeyer, whose Auto Union averaged 82.5mph to win; in second and third places respectively were Dick Seaman (Mercedes) and American, Rex Mays (Alfa Romeo).

In Detroit, the United Auto Workers union had settled a running dispute with GM. However, there were riots following labor disputes at Ford and US Steel.

But there were triumphs too in 1937, among them being the opening of the Golden Gate Bridge across San Francisco Bay. This stately suspension bridge with its soaring towers was a masterpiece of engineering that remains as impressive today as it was 60 years ago.

While many buyers of automobiles that year would have marveled at the Golden Gate Bridge, a significant number of them were also impressed by the new LaSalle. With a longer wheelbase and a V8 engine, the car was snapped up and production rose to a record level. Total Cadillac production that year was 46,000 cars, and LaSalle accounted for 32,000 of them.

Interestingly, the styling of the '37 LaSalle could be traced back to 1934, when it had

Below: In 1934, the restyled LaSalle had been chosen as official pace car for the Indy 500 race. That honor was bestowed on the marque again for 1937, when a convertible coupe led the procession around the famous track. Although originally styled in 1934, and with only minor changes since, the LaSalle had a graceful, streamlined appearance that in no way looked dated.

definitely been ahead of its time. The car received a completely new look in 1934, following a poor showing in the early part of the decade. While the car had originally been conceived to fill the gap between the bottom-of-the-range Cadillacs and the top-of-the-range Buicks, by the beginning of the Thirties, there was not much to choose between it and the less expensive Cadillacs. Although the difference in price was about $500 (a substantial sum in those days), the Cadillacs actually seemed to provide better value for money, and their production outstripped LaSalle.

Rather than drop the LaSalle line altogether, GM executives decided to give it a more positive identity so that it was no longer perceived as simply a cheap Cadillac and, therefore, would appeal to a wider audience, other than the traditional buyers of luxury cars. LaSalle could trade on the prestige of being associated with Cadillac and the upmarket body builders Fleetwood, but there would be no doubt that it was not a Cadillac. Moreover, this was emphasized by the $1000 price difference between the LaSalle and the bottom-of-the-line Caddy.

The new streamlined body style had many features that would not be found on other automobiles until later in the decade. Among these were airfoil-shaped fenders that were full and low at the front, blending into the radiator shell and concealing the frame rails. The teardrop-shaped headlights were supported on the radiator shell and the grille was tall, narrow and oval. The hood sides featured a line of oval ports rather than the normal louvers. The windshield was raked to match the sloping grille and the doors were all of the suicide type, hinged at the rear.

Body styles comprised 4-door sedan, club sedan and convertible sedan, and 2-door coupe and convertible coupe. These were all mounted on a new X-frame chassis with a wheelbase of 119 inches. GM's new "Knee-Action" coil-sprung independent front suspension was adopted, while semi-elliptic leaf springs supported the rear Hotchkiss drive, which replaced Cadillac's more traditional torque-tube arrangement. Double-action shock absorbers were fitted all round, while a rear stabilizer bar was also incorporated to improve ride and handling. Unlike Cadillacs that year, the LaSalles benefited from Bendix hydraulic brakes.

During the early Thirties, LaSalles had been given Cadillac's 353 cu.in. V8, but the new model had Oldsmobile's 240.3 cu.in. flat-head straight-eight with aluminum pistons and five main bearings. It produced 95 horsepower (10 less than the V8) at 3700rpm and was backed by a three-speed manual transmission, also of Oldsmobile design. At the time, however, Cadillac were keen to conceal the source of the engine and other driveline parts, stating that they were built at the Cadillac factory, and they were prepared to

Left: Ab Jenkins had long been a proponent of Bonneville Salt Flats as a venue for automobile record attempts, and he ran a number of cars there during the Thirties. In 1937, he drove this Cord in a 24-hour endurance run, during which he reached a speed of 101.72mph.

Below: Chevrolets for 1937 received all new Diamond Crown styling with pinched-in grilles, revised fenders and body side molding that ran back from the fenders into the doors. Safety glass was fitted to all cars, which were based on a 112¼ inch wheelbase and were powered by 216.5 cu.in. ohv six cylinder engines. A wide range of body styles was offered in Master (shown) and Master Deluxe form. The former came with a single tail light and single windshield wiper, while there were no front fender parking lights.

allow potential customers to visit the factory to see for themselves. Of course, the individual parts may have actually been made by Oldsmobile and simply assembled by Cadillac.

The cars continued in this basic form for 1935 and 1936 with minor changes to styling and mechanical components. For example, the wheelbase was increased to 120 inches and all cars received a two-piece, V-shaped windshield. The engine was also bored out to give a capacity of 248 cu.in. and produce 105 horsepower at 3600rpm. The bodies were no longer built by Fleetwood, as production had been transferred to Fisher, who produced a new all-steel turret roof for closed cars.

Again, for 1937, styling changes were minimal, although the wheelbase had been stretched to 124 inches and the bodies were all-steel rather than of composite wood-and-steel construction. Changes included revisions to the front fenders, lowering of the head lights, a new "egg-crate" grille and a windshield with a deeper V-shape. The hood side ports had also been dropped in favor of a line of deep rectangular louvers with horizontal moldings running through them.

A choice of five body styles was offered: 2- and 4-door sedans, a convertible sedan, a convertible coupe and a sport coupe.

The big news that year, however, was the return of a V8 engine. This 322 cu.in. flathead produced 125 horsepower at 3400rpm and

had been used in the previous year's Cadillac Series 60. The three-speed manual transmission remained, but the Hotchkiss drive was replaced by a hypoid unit. A stabilizer was also added to the front suspension.

The improvements transformed the car, and sales took off. Sadly, a minor recession in 1938 would cause them to fall again. Minor changes had been made to the cars for that year, including mounting the headlights on the tops of the fenders, but they were hung off the radiator shell again in 1939. LaSalles received several other changes that year, too, including increased glass area, a new narrower grille, and a steel sunroof, known as the "Sunshine Turret Top", for sedans. Running boards were optional. The wheelbase that year was back to 120 inches but, even so, sales remained uninspiring.

By 1940, the Buick range had expanded upwards, catering for the market originally conceived for LaSalle. Despite new elegant body styling and a wider range of models than before, this competition, together with the fact that LaSalle was being pressed hard by Lincoln and lagging well behind Packard, meant that 1940 would be the last year for LaSalles. The name would appear again briefly in the mid Fifties on a couple of GM concept cars but, other than that, it would be consigned to history. However, LaSalles would always be remembered as distinctive and refined automobiles.

Above: Hudsons received a significant restyle for 1937. Bodies were widened and lowered, while wheelbases were increased. However, the distinctive "waterfall" grille remained, albeit in a simpler form compared to earlier models. A wide range of body styles was offered in six and eight cylinder versions. The former could have a choice of 101 or 107 horsepower, 212 cu.in. flathead straight-six engines, while the latter had a 122 horsepower, 254.47 cu.in. straight-eight.

1938

Unlike the previous year, 1938 proved a good one for aviation when millionaire Howard Hughes made history by flying his twin-engined Beech airplane around the world in a record time of 3 days, 19 hours and 17 minutes. He wasn't the only one remembered for achieving a remarkable feat that year. Orson Wells caused mass panic across the US, with his broadcast of "The War of the Worlds" radio play, and thousands of Americans truly believed their country was under attack from alien spaceships. They need not have worried because, as anyone picking up Action Comics' first edition would have found, Superman also made his debut.

Among the technological achievements that year was the invention of the Xerox photocopier by Chester Carlton, and the development of nylon products by Du Pont. Teflon and fiber glass also made their appearance.

Although some auto makers were noted for technological innovation, Packard was not one of them. Nevertheless, their cars offered refined luxury, a timeless appeal, and good performance. During the Thirties, the bodies of their cars had become more streamlined in keeping with general styling trends but, even in 1938, they were still using an upright grille design that had been introduced in the early part of the decade. However, that did not matter, as it suited the elegant image of the cars. Packard were at the top end of the market, producing low-volume, carefully-built cars for the wealthier, more discerning buyer.

Given their potential market, the Packard range of 1938 was surprisingly comprehensive, offering a wide choice of models and body styles. These included a six cylinder series, two eight cylinder series and a twelve cylinder series. Although in styling, the cars appeared similar to the 1937 models, there were substantial changes. The previous flat, one-piece windshield was replaced with a two-piece V-shaped windshield on all series and, in addition, all body styles had pontoon fenders, which partially enveloped the side-mount spares where these were fitted.

At the bottom of the Packard range was the Packard Six which, for 1938, received a 7 inch increase of wheelbase taking it to 122 inches. The chassis was fitted with a completely new, all-steel body, rather than the composite wood-and-steel of previous years. Although eventually all car bodies would be

Left: Packards form the basis for many custom body packages. This Greber is a typical example. Unlike production '38 Packards, its radiator shell and surrounding "catwalk" has been chromed. The pelican emblem on top of the shell was a $10 dollar option in 1938.

Above: Along with the twelve cylinder models, the Super Eights were the top-of-the-line Packards in 1938. They offered elegance and performance in a variety of body styles ranging from coupe to limousine.

Above: In 1938, Graham introduced a unique body style which they called the "Spirit of Motion". This incorporated faired-in head lights and a forward-leaning radiator grille that became known as the sharknose. Four sedans were offered, all of them 4-door models based on a 120 inch wheelbase chassis with a six cylinder engine. Two were supercharged. Coupe and 2-door sedans were added for 1939, but the design proved too radical and sales were poor.

Right: Ab Jenkins was back at the Bonneville Salt Flats with the massive Mormon Meteor II, seeking yet more endurance records. The venerable streamlined car was powered by an Allison V12 airplane engine, and had been used by Jenkins in a number of record attempts throughout the Thirties. During the course of 1938's 24-hour dash, he broke a total of 87 speed records.

built totally from steel, this method of manufacture caused problems when first used. Until advances were made in sound-deadening materials, all-steel bodies sounded cheap and tinny when doors were slammed. Wooden framed bodies had a more solid-sound and so were retained for more expensive cars in order to exude an air of quality.

Compared to 1937, the Six was offered in fewer body styles, with five in total: business coupe, 2+2 club coupe, convertible coupe, and 2- and 4-door sedans. All were powered by Packard's flathead, in-line six cylinder engine, which had been bored out to 3½ inches to give a displacement of 245 cu.in. While there was no increase in horsepower (100), torque was improved and giving a top speed of 78mph. To aid cooling, the engine was also equipped with an improved water pump and fan, and radiator capacity was increased.

Like all other Packards that year, the Six featured three-speed synchromesh transmission, Safe-T-fleX independent front suspension and hydraulic brakes, the last two having been introduced for 1937.

A step up from the Six was the Eight, which had been known as the One Twenty in 1937. This also received a 7 inch increase in wheelbase (to 127 inches), while long wheelbase limousine and sedan versions were set at 148 inches. Eleven body styles were offered in this series, three of which featured beauti-

ful custom coachwork by Rollston: an all-weather cabriolet, an all-weather town car and an all-weather brougham. The remainder comprised two coupes, a convertible coupe, a convertible sedan, a 2- and a 4-door sedan, a limousine and a long wheelbase sedan. The 4-door sedan came in standard and Deluxe versions, although a wide list of optional accessories made it possible to give any of the body styles a de luxe specification.

The Packard Eight had a flathead in-line eight cylinder engine that displaced 282 cu.in. and developed 120 horsepower at 3800rpm. This engine had been used in 1937 but, for 1938, the compression ratio was raised from 6.5 to 6.6:1. An optional aluminum head increased compression to 7.05:1.

A similar, but larger, engine was fitted to the Super Eight series which, together with the Twelves, provided the top-of-the-range models. In the Super Eight, the straight eight engine displaced 320 cu.in. and produced 130 horsepower at 3200rpm. Otherwise, it was similar mechanically to the other Packards.

Based on three sizes of chassis, with wheelbases of 127, 134 and 139 inches, the Super Eight offered a choice of 17 body styles. These included four custom-built models by outside coachbuilders: Rollston produced an all-weather cabriolet and a town car, while Brunn made another all-weather cabriolet and a touring cabriolet. The remainder of the range included a variety of sedan specifications, among them a touring sedan with a removable roof section over the driving compartment. There were also coupes, convertibles and limousines.

A wide variety of accessories was offered with the Super Eight, with some provided in packages such as the Custom Accessory Group and the Deluxe Accessory Group. One new accessory for that year was the guest speaker – a radio speaker which fitted into the back of the driver's seat to ensure a perfect reception for back-seat passengers. An extra $10 bought the company's pelican emblem for the top of the radiator grille.

The twelve cylinder cars had much in common with the Super Eight, having the same body changes compared to the 1937 models and sharing the same three chassis. These were the really expensive Packards – not only to buy, but also to run with their 473.3 cu.in. 175 horsepower, flathead V12 engines. The cheapest Twelve – a 2+2 coupe, cost $4135, while the equivalent Super Eight went for $2925. Not surprisingly, relatively few Twelves (566) were sold. By 1939, the car would only be built to order and, thereafter, was dropped from the Packard line-up.

Despite the fact that Twelves were expensive cars, 14 body styles were listed, including the same custom packages offered by Rollston and Brunn on the Super Eight. Their mechanical specification was much the same as the other Packard series, but because of the extra weight of the V12 engine, the braking system had vacuum assistance.

Post-war, Packards would lose much of their regal look as the company strove to

move into mass production. Although there would be technical innovation, the glorious years of Packard style would always remain pre-war, and the 1938 models are typical of the era.

Above: All new-look '38 Hudsons had a simpler grille. The Terraplane models had a "waterfall" central divider echoing that of the '37 models, and were based on a 117 inch wheelbase.

1939

As America celebrated the arrival of a new year on the eve of 1939, in Europe the ominous clouds of war were gathering. Later in the year, the storm would break: German Chancellor Adolf Hitler would send his troops into Czechoslovakia, then Poland, prompting Great Britain and France to declare war on Germany. This was the beginning of a terrible conflict that eventually would span continents and last for six long years.

Although the United States took a neutral stance at this stage of the war and would not take a belligerent role until after the Japanese strike on Pearl Harbor in 1941, under President Roosevelt, she increasingly provided military aid of all kinds to the Allies, in particular the British. Without America's assistance in this way, the events of the early years of the war might have taken another direction altogether.

Helping to cement the special relationship between the US and Great Britain, King George VI and Queen Elizabeth toured the United States in 1939. Although they would cross the Atlantic by ship, other travelers could take advantage of a more rapid means of travel, for that year saw the inauguration of Pan American's regular transatlantic air service, which made use of Boeing Clipper flying boats.

To escape the dreary news from Europe – and at home, where the economy remained stagnant – Americans could take in a movie and see Clark Gable in "Gone With The Wind", or Judy Garland in the "Wizard of Oz". Or they could visit the World's Fair, which had opened in New York.

"Economy" was a word that also played a major part in some of Ford's advertising that year, although in a different context. In an attempt to compete with the top-of-the-range Oldsmobiles and Dodges, and lower-range Buicks and Chryslers, Ford had launched a completely new model range for 1939 under the Mercury name. The new cars – a convertible, a coupe, a 2-door sedan and a 4-door town sedan – fitted neatly between the standard Ford offerings and the much more luxurious and larger Lincoln Zephyrs. Their overall styling was similar to both the Lincoln Zephyr and the de luxe Fords, but at 116 inches, the wheelbase was 9 inches shorter than the former and 4 inches longer than the latter. Apart from the slightly larger size, the

immediate identifying feature between the Mercury and Ford was that the Mercury had horizontal grille bars, while the de luxe Fords had vertical bars. The Mercury coupe also had a distinctive roofline and side glass both of which were quite different from those of the Ford.

Mechanically, the Mercury was similar in construction to the Ford, but from the outset it was fitted with Lockheed hydraulic brakes, whereas both the Ford and Lincoln Zephyr had only switched to hydraulics that year. It was powered by a 95 horsepower version of Ford's famous flathead V8, and it soon gained a reputation as being a hot performer for a big car. Despite this, Ford emphasized the fuel economy of the Mercury, which they claimed could be as much as 20 miles to the gallon and which few cars of any size could match at the time.

Like most of Ford's products, the Mercury sold very well from the outset, establishing the Mercury name, which would continue in the company's line-up from then on. A slight increase in the size of the wheelbase, to 118 inches, would follow in 1940 and the cars would continue to sell well until all civilian automobile production was stopped at the beginning of 1942 to devote capacity to the war effort. Up to that time, the Mercury had always been regarded as an upmarket Ford. However, after the war was over, the parent company would form the Lincoln-Mercury division, and all future Mercurys would be offered as the less expensive versions of the company's luxury cars, rather than the more luxurious forms of their bread-and-butter auto-mobile range.

Above left: At a glance, the Mercury town sedan looked similar to the 4-door Ford, with the same roofline, hood and fender shape. However, the horizontal grille bars are unmistakable.

Far left: Studebaker's Champion series arrived in 1939. Powered by an in-line flathead six, this Deluxe sedan came with broadcloth upholstery, quarter windows and dual windshield wipers.

Left: Willys-Overland spent much of the Thirties in receivership, but by 1939 the company was back on its feet, introducing the four cylinder, 48 horsepower model 48.

1940

As 1940 progressed, the news from Europe was increasingly gloomy; France, Belgium and the Low Countries all fell to Germany. Meanwhile, the British had managed to evacuate most of their expeditionary force from Dunkirk. After a short lull, the German airforce began to attack targets in Britain in preparation for the expected invasion; the Battle of Britain had begun and would rage throughout the summer. Against all odds, the RAF inflicted substantial damage on the German airforce, such that they could not guarantee control of the air, which was essential for a successful seaborne invasion. Germany had experienced her first setback of the war.

Roosevelt, who would be elected as President for a third term, was in constant contact with Prime Minister Winston Churchill. At his urging, America moved from a policy of neutrality to one of non-belligerence, and much of industry, particularly the auto industry, began to take on the production of armaments and other military equipment. Even so, substantial numbers of new automobiles were still produced. Buick broke their annual production record, exceeding 250,116 cars, and also built their 4,000,000th automobile.

Following the recession of 1938, Buick's President, Harlow Curtice, had ordered a 10% reduction in material and component costs across the board. When it came to the chassis of the small series cars, this was achieved by removing the portion that overhung the back axle. This rear section was considered unnecessary as Buick had switched from parallel leaf springs, which needed a mounting behind the axle, to coil springs that did not. Pre-production testing had shown no problems, but once the cars began to reach the public, collapsed trunk floors and distorted bodies caused by minor parking bumps were reported. The only solution was to restore the rear portion of the frame and rush out a reinforcing framework to be fitted to existing cars. This proved both costly and embarrassing.

As a result, Curtice eased financial restrictions on the 1940 models, which received even more rigorous testing than normal, covering nearly 3,000,000 miles of cross-country driving. The resulting new cars were traditional with proven engineering.

The cars shared their general styling with the 1939 models, but received a face-lift that saw the head lights blended into the front fenders, and a wider grille with horizontal rather than vertical bars. In all, there were six series: Special Series 40, Super Series 50, Century Series 60, Roadmaster Series 70, Limited Series 80 and Limited Series 90. All shared the same front-end styling, but their wheelbase varied from 121 inches for the 40 and 50, through 126 inches for the 60 and 70, to 133 inches for the 80 and 140 inches for the 90. These sizes were common to the '39

Below: The Lincoln Continental was a new model for 1940, being based on the Lincoln Zephyr mechanicals and the established flathead V12 engine. New, stylish bodywork was developed that was 3 inches lower than the Lincoln Zephyr and had a hood that was 7 inches longer. Coupe and cabriolet (illustrated) models were offered.

Left: Bottom of the Buick range were the Special Series 40 models. In addition to the 4-door sedan shown, the series included a 2-door sedan, a 4-door phaeton, a 2-door convertible, a business coupe, a sport coupe and a taxi. The parking lights above the head lights could be wired into the directional signal system

models, but the Series 40 and 50 cars enjoyed a 1 inch increase to allow enough room for the front doors of cars, equipped with sidemount spares, to open fully! In addition, Series 50 and 70 cars were devoid of running boards.

Buick's range encompassed mid-priced bread-and-butter models and upmarket luxury cars that encroached upon the Cadillac market, which did not endear them to their fellow GM division. However, the top-of-the-range

cars gave much kudos to the less-expensive models, the entire range having an air of quality. All the cars were powered by Buick's trusty ohv straight-eight engine, of either 248 or 320.2 cu.in., depending on the series. This was backed by a three-speed manual transmission with torque-tube drive to the rear axle. Oil filters were standard as were sealed-beam headlights, while a new option was Fore-N-Aft Flash-Way directional signals.

Right: The tiny Crosley had appeared in 1939, the brainchild of Powel Crosley who had made a fortune in the manufacture of radios and refrigerators. Powered by an air-cooled, twin-cylinder engine that developed 15 horsepower, it came in convertible coupe, convertible sedan and station wagon versions, all based on an 80 inch wheelbase. Driveline and motor mount problems caused sales to plummet in 1940, but they picked up again in 1941 after the defects had been cured. Post-war, the Crosley was fitted with an ohc four cylinder engine and enjoyed a considerable following.

1941

By 1941, most of Europe was under the German jackboot; only Great Britain stood defiant, but bloodied, refusing to be subdued. Through the lend-lease scheme, America was providing military equipment and supplies to the embattled British, despite officially being non-belligerent. As an explanation, President Roosevelt argued that if there had been a fire in his neighbor's house he would have lent that neighbor a hose to put it out. In addition to actual equipment, the US also provided naval escorts for convoys carrying it across the Atlantic, helping to protect it from U-boat attack. Moreover, the US Navy and Coast Guard mounted their own anti-submarine patrols to protect Allied vessels when entering and leaving American ports.

Although Britain was holding out against German aggression, British Prime Minister, Winston Churchill, knew that there was no chance of turning the tide of the war against the German forces. He needed the USA to declare war on Germany, but America had not been attacked, nor were there any treaties that bound her to come to the aid of any victims of German aggression. That situation would change at the end of the year.

At the start of 1941, despite the ominous rumblings from across the Atlantic, it was business as usual for Detroit. At Chrysler, it was a face-lift year, the new models being similar in appearance to the 1940 offerings, although the bodies were wider and the cars had a lower stance. A six-bar grille replaced the previous year's nine-bar unit, and the cars could be ordered with or without running boards. Ever since the lack of success achieved by the radically-styled Airflow model which appeared in 1934, the overall

Right: Although not spectacular, Chrysler's styling for 1941 projected the company's dependable image and steady progress through proven engineering. The standard transmission for all models was the Fluid Drive semi-automatic.

Above: Oldsmobile's three series offered a wide range of models, all with a choice of six or eight cylinder in-line engines. Their styling was similar to the previous year's offerings, but the wheelbase was longer. This is a Series 60 4-door, five-passenger sedan.

styling of Chryslers had been conservative and, for 1941, the cars followed their rather staid image. However, in engineering terms, the company was always innovative.

The '41 models had a similar mechanical specification to their predecessors, the standard transmission being Chrysler's Fluid Drive, which had been in production for a couple of years. This was an unusual three-speed, semi-automatic transmission that incorporated a clutch mechanism. The clutch was used to select first gear, after which the pedal was released fully, then the accelerator depressed to move off, just like a normal automatic. Once on the move, the driver selected second gear by simply lifting his foot from the accelerator, yet when shifting into third, the clutch had to be used in the same way as with a manual transmission. Down-shifting was achieved in a similar manner.

Although the technique sounds confusing, at the time Chrysler advertised Fluid Drive as being the transmission you could not make a mistake with. Obviously, plenty of people agreed, as the cars sold well.

Chryslers offered in 1941 were available in two basic series: 28 and 30. The former

was powered by a new "Spitfire" sidevalve in-line six engine, which had a capacity of 241.5 cu.in. and came in low- and high-compression versions that produced 108 and 112 horse-power respectively, although the latter was increased to 115 horsepower later in the year. The 30 series models were equipped with a sidevalve in-line eight cylinder engine, which displaced 323.5 cu.in. and produced either 137 (low compression) or 140 horse-power (high compression) at 3400 rpm. The hood of these eight cylinder cars was slightly longer to accommodate the engine.

Within the two series was a wide range of styles, including coupes, convertibles, 2-door broughams, 4-door sedans, station wagons and long wheelbase limousines. These were sold as Royal, Windsor, Saratoga, New Yorker and Crown Imperial models.

Among the options available was a striking upholstery pattern, which cost an extra $20 and was similar to Black Watch tartan. This fancy stitchwork led to a completely separate series of Windsor and New Yorker models, known as Highlanders. To distinguish them they carried Highlander emblems on the dashboard and hood.

Despite Chrysler's less-than-flamboyant image, buyers in 1941 could choose from a list of 13 colors and 27 upholstery options. Also included in the list of options was a four-speed, semi-automatic transmission known as Vacamatic, and power-operated windows, although the latter were only available on the top-of-the-line Crown Imperial.

Compared to their poor performance during the recession of 1938, Chrysler were doing well in 1941, having more than tripled their sales. They were ranked eighth in the US auto industry that year, but still fell a long way behind Oldsmobile in sixth place, who built their 2,000,000th automobile in 1941.

The Oldsmobile range of 1941 comprised three series – 60, 70 and 90 – as it had done in 1940 and, while they appeared similar in styling, in fact they were all based on longer wheelbase chassis. Bottom-of-the-range 60 series cars grew 3 inches to 119 inches, while the 70 and 90 series shared a 125 inch wheelbase from 120 and 124 inches respectively).

All three series of cars could be specified with either a 238 cu.in. in-line flathead six or 257 cu.in. eight, being designated 66 or 68, 76 or 78, or 96 or 98 as appropriate. In fact, 1941 was the only year in which a top-of-the-line 90 series car could be ordered with a six, but few buyers took up the option and it was not offered again. What they did go for, however, was the Hydramatic automatic transmission.

The three series offered a range of body styles, including convertibles, business and club coupes, 2- and 4-door sedans and station wagons. An unusual offering was a 4-door phaeton, which had been introduced in 1940, but would be discontinued after 1941.

1941 was a good year for the auto makers and few realized what was in store for them. Indeed, few Americans had any inkling of what was to come until 7th December, when the Japanese launched a devastating surprise attack on the Pacific Fleet, based at Pearl Harbor in the Hawaiian Islands. In a furious air assault, they virtually destroyed the Pacific Fleet, torpedoing five battleships and two cruisers within the first few minutes. Fortunately, two aircraft carriers were at sea when the attack took place and would prove to be a valuable nucleus around which a new fleet could be built. In the meantime, however, Japan would be almost unchallenged in her conquest of much of the Pacific.

America was now at war with Japan, and because the latter was part of a tripartite pact with Germany and Italy (the Axis powers), at war with those countries, too. The Japanese also struck at British-held Singapore, while the Germans gave up trying to crack Great Britain and turned their attention east to the

Soviet Union, ignoring the non-aggression pact they had signed with that country. All the elements were in place for a world conflict, but both Germany and Japan had awakened sleeping giants which, ultimately, would cause their downfall.

Now all of American industry had to turn its attention to the war effort. Automobile production was cut by 20% as the factories began producing military equipment. Soon they would be making nothing else as America concentrated her entire might on the common cause.

Above: The Nash Ambassador 600 pioneered unitized body and frame construction for 1941. Powered by a 172.6cu.in. flathead six, there were eight models, including coupes, a brougham and 2- and 4-door sedans.

Below: Sedans were available in all three series of Oldsmobile, but they did not share the same body style. This Series 70 has a sloping fastback body whereas the Series 60 on the facing page is a notchback.

1942

By the beginning of 1942, the Japanese were making steady progress in their conquest of the Pacific islands, while American industry was turning rapidly to war production. As a result, many raw materials were severely restricted for civilian use and some withdrawn completely. From 1 January, the government had banned brightwork on cars, with the exception of bumpers, bumper guards and windshield wipers. Such automobiles had their trim painted a contrasting color and were popularly known as "black-out specials". Then, from 2 February, the production of civilian cars and trucks was banned completely – America was committed to total war.

With production curtailed so early in the year, few new models reached civilian hands and potential buyers had to prove a specific need for a car. Most were impressed for military service, including Chevrolet's face-lift model for 1942. Based on the previous year's design, using the same chassis, mechanical components and basic body shell, the updated Chevy appeared longer, wider and lower, yet the wheelbase remained the same at 116 inches. The new look was achieved by installing a more prominent radiator grille, by stretching the hood back to the leading edge of the doors, and by extending the front fenders well into the doors; the rear portion of the fender, known as a fender cap, opened with the door. From there back, the car was essentially the same as the 1941 model.

Chevrolet's two model lines – Special Deluxe and Master Deluxe – included sedans, coupes and cabriolets. The Special Deluxe versions had a few extra accessories to set them apart from the others. In 1941, a close-coupled 4-door sedan, the Fleetline, had been

the top of the range but, for 1942, it was upstaged by the sleeker, fastback Fleetline Aerosedan. This attractive 2-door body style had a low roofline that swept down in a continuous curve to the rear bumper. As a result, the windshield and side glass were shorter, and the seats were lower too. Both Fleetline models were distinguished by three stainless-steel moldings on each fender, but otherwise they were similarly equipped to the other Special Deluxe models.

Power for all '42 Chevies came from the trusty "stovebolt" in-line-six engine, the basic design of which had been in use since 1937. It displaced 216.5 cubic inches, had a 6.5:1 compression ratio and pumped out 90 horsepower. Chevrolet continued to use this same engine in their post-war models until 1953.

Despite the relatively short time that it was available, the Fleetline Aerosedan proved a winner, outselling all other Chevrolet models. Nearly 62,000 were built before production was halted in February. For the rest of the year, Chevrolet concentrated on building military trucks. However, the fastback Aerosedan styling would return after the war and continue in the Chevrolet line-up until 1952.

Although the lack of new cars and the advent of sugar and gasoline rationing made life less comfortable, not all the news of 1942 was bad. At the cinema, Humphrey Bogart and Ingrid Bergman were starring in the classic film "Casablanca", while on stage, a young skinny guy by the name of Frank Sinatra was keeping the kids happy. On the war front, the Japanese navy had been severely mauled at the Battle of Midway in early June, losing several valuable aircraft carriers, General Dwight D. Eisenhower had been named commander of American forces in Europe, and those forces began to prove themselves when they invaded North Africa in November to harass German troops retreating from Britain's Eighth Army. This crucial amphibious assault was to be useful practice for the invasion of Europe, still two years away.

Right: Santa Claus may well have been able to prove his need for a new 1942 model at the end of 1941, but for those Americans who couldn't, owning a Chevrolet Fleetline Aerosedan such as this was simply a dream. Built before the beginning of the model year, this model has all its brightwork intact.

Below: As the 1942 models were announced, it was clear that sleek lines were the order of the day. This beautiful Buick Roadmaster Model 71 convertible was a prime example. Long and low, its lines were accentuated by sweeping, flow-through fenders, fender skirts, wraparound bumpers and parallel moldings running the length of the lower body.

Below: The Hudson's 1942 model, with its simpler, lower grille and hidden running boards, was an attractive car. A choice of in-line six- or eight-cylinder engines was offered.

1943–45

After the dark days of 1942, 1943 was to see America and the other Allied nations pursuing the war against Germany and Japan with vigor. With the wealth of American manpower and industry behind it, the allied war effort was slowly making gains. In Europe, Allied troops invaded Italy as a prelude to the far more critical invasion of northern Europe – D Day – in 1944. In the Pacific, Japan's island conquests were wrested back one by one. Of course, there were setbacks, as the aggressors fought tooth and nail to retain the lands that they had seized. But progress on both fronts was inexorable. German forces would eventually be fought to a standstill by US, British and other Allied armies in the west and Soviet troops in the east, capitulating at the beginning of May 1945. Japan followed suit in August after Hiroshima and Nagasaki were devastated by atomic bombs.

Throughout this time, the American automobile industry backed the war effort to the hilt. Not only did they build trucks, but also many of their factories were turned over to the production of other military equipment. Ford built B-24 bombers and tanks; Chevrolet, airplane engines and guns; Cadillac and Buick made tanks and airplane engines; Packard and Studebaker built engines for airplanes and torpedo boats;

Pontiac and Oldsmobile manufactured canon and anti-aircraft guns.

Throughout this period, however, a "car" was still being built, although its purpose, not surprisingly, was purely military. In the army's parlance, it was known as a "¼-ton, 4x4 truck", but it soon became affectionately, and officially, known as the Jeep. It was built by the hundreds of thousand and served in every theater of the war. The axis powers had nothing like it; nor indeed had there ever been anything like it. The Jeep was a lightweight, rugged, powerful, go-anywhere vehicle that served both on and off the battlefield. Without doubt, it was the most versatile vehicle of WW2. It could be used for reconnaissance missions, running supplies to front-line troops, evacuating wounded, towing artillery pieces, carrying radio equipment, transporting generals, and myriad other tasks. Equipped with machine guns, it was used for hit-and-run raids behind enemy lines; it was landed by glider with airborne forces. It could negotiate thick mud, climb steep inclines and ford deep water.

Designed by Willys-Overland to meet the requirements of the US Army for a lightweight scout car, the Jeep had a strong chassis and simple open bodywork with no doors and a fold-flat windshield. It could seat three, but in

Right: "Tough as nails. Fast as lightning. Dependable as the fighting men who man them – Willys-built Jeeps are sparking the attack of American and Allied fighting forces in every thundering theater of war". So ran a Willys advertisement during WW2. It was apt, too, for the versatile Jeep provided ground troops with go-anywhere mobility.

action it often carried many more. Its 134.2 cu.in. four cylinder engine developed 60 horsepower and was backed by a four-speed transmission with high and low ranges; two- or four-wheel-drive could be selected at will. The result was a vehicle with good highway speed (in excess of 60mph) and real stump-pulling power to deal with rough terrain.

To guard their source of supply during wartime, the military insisted that Jeeps be built by at least one other manufacturer, but that they be identical in every respect so that parts were interchangeable. The masters of mass-production, Ford, were given this role and built many thousands of the little vehicles.

The one controversial aspect of the Jeep is how it got its name. No one seems to know for sure. Some argue that it came about from its military designation, GP (General Purpose); others say that it was named after a character in the Popeye cartoon strip. Whatever the truth may be, the fact is that the Jeep not only helped win the war, but also was the forerunner of a whole line of four-wheel-drive vehicles (both military and civilian) that has continued to this day.

Above: While Willys and Ford were building Jeeps, other automobile manufacturers made trucks or devoted their engineering resources to other military needs. Chrysler, for example, developed their Fluid Drive automatic transmission for naval use. Throughout the war, the automobile industry advertised the role it was playing in the war effort, keeping their names in front of the public, no doubt with post-war sales in mind.

Left: The Jeep was a no-frills, effective military vehicle. From every angle, it is a purposeful design. It was used by all the Allied forces and was looked upon with affection by the men who came to depend upon it. There is no doubt that it made a major contribution to victory on all fronts.

1946

Emerging from the war, most manufacturers could only offer revamped 1942 models to the eagerly-awaiting public. It didn't matter. As long as it had four wheels and an engine, you could find a buyer willing to exchange their savings for it. This pent-up demand gave false hopes to quite a few entrepreneurs who attempted to enter what appeared to be an extremely lucrative business – most of these newcomers ended up losing their shirts.

But if the cars seemed familiar, much else had changed since Pearl Harbor. Global conflict led to huge advances in technology and America was propelled into the atomic era, with jets, rockets and computers. These space age influences would form themes in every automobile produced in the USA (and beyond) but, for now, a more conservative approach was necessary to get cars delivered to customers as quickly as possible.

There could be few more traditional people in the industry than Chrysler president K. T. Keller (the initials stood for Kaufman Thuma, but nobody ever dared use those names) who had taken over the reigns from Walter P. Chrysler in 1935. Keller's concept of car design was firmly rooted in the past, as can be judged by part of a talk he gave in 1947: "Automobiles are looked at and admired. The buyer is proud of his car's symphony of line; its coloring and trim express his taste; he welcomes the applause of his friends and neighbors. But he bought the car to ride in, and for his wife, and children, and friends to ride in... Though at times one might wonder, even headroom is important. Many of you Californians may have outgrown of the habit, but there are parts of the country, containing millions of people, where both the men and the ladies are in the habit of getting behind the wheel, or in the back seat, wearing hats."

Engineering took precedence over styling at Chrysler, and maintaining sufficient clearance for headgear obviously restricted the designer's options, resulting in a rather more upright look than most other cars. One commentator described the early 1940s Chrysler body thus: "It won't knock your socks off, but it won't knock your hat off, either".

And it is from this rather staid background that the magnificent Town & Country model was born. As the woodwork suggests, its origins lay with a station wagon, but not the usual rectangular timber box built on the back

of a sedan body. It was David A. Wallace, general manager at Chrysler, who decided to add a station wagon to the catalog – a model new to them. However, Wallace specified a wagon with the curved lines of a sedan and this somewhat perplexed the bodybuilders who normally manufactured the "woodies".

Faced with reluctance, Wallace decided to bring the project in house and gave the problem to his own team of engineers. The solution was arrived at after much hard work and,

1946

Left: The convertible Town & Country provided some much needed glamor to boost an otherwise conservative selection of Chrysler post-war autos. The company was then dominated by the engineering aspect of a car's design and styling tended to be of secondary consideration. By far the most expensive Chrysler model for 1946, at nearly $3,000, only 1,935 ragtops were produced that year.

in 1941, the first Town & Country station wagons were produced at the Jefferson Avenue plant in Detroit by a group of skilled workers who learned the techniques required for mating metal and wood in such close harmony. About 1,000 cars were made in the first year, followed by a similar number in 1942.

Chrysler's sales team concluded that it wasn't the practical aspect of the wagon that attracted customers, but its unique appearance and the elegant mix of steel, white ash and mahogany. Accordingly, it was decided to create a whole new luxurious selection of Town & County models utilizing the striking wood features. Although several prototypes were built of varying body styles, only two versions were to make it into production – a 4-door sedan and a 2-door convertible.

Mounted on a 127.5 inch wheelbase New Yorker chassis and powered by the 323 cu.in. L-head straight eight coupled to a Fluid-Drive transmission, the handsome Town & Country ragtop established a uniquely American model style. By far the most expensive Chrysler model for 1946, at nearly three thousand dollars, only 1,935 were produced that year.

Chrysler used such words as 'thoroughbred' to describe the Town & Country in their advertisements; the car was shown in opulent surroundings as befitted such a model. At the sailing club, driving through big iron gates at the entrance to a colonnaded mansion or on the archery range – these were the settings chosen to add the much-needed glamor to an otherwise fairly unremarkable range of cars.

The text accompanying the illustrations could be equally fulsome: "Chrysler's work or play convertible...magnificent in its utterly new styling..." ran an early advert, and later copy was even bolder: "...the industry's most dramatic, most exciting, most daring styling. A classic of the long, low, and lovely – with the most luxurious trim... With beauty that truly reflects the inspired and sound engineering and solid comfort inside."

Stylist Raymond Dietrich was warned about the emphasis placed on the engineering aspect of Chrysler products when he joined in 1932. Although he was to leave Chrysler in 1940, after yet another dispute with head of engineering, Fred Zeder, the foundation of the 1946 Town & Country design seems to have come from Dietrich with the contours of the 1941 models. Robert Cadwallader took over as head of design after Dietrich's departure, with Herb Weissinger and Arnott 'Buzz' Grisinger playing major roles in styling.

Describing the situation following the end of the war, as manufacturers scrambled to resume production, Grisinger recalled in a later interview: "Postwar plans were pretty much a hurry-up thing. There weren't any clay models or production prototypes... We just designed a series of different styles and brushed on wood trim where we thought it looked best. Sales took it from there."

Aside from the "brushed on" wood trim, the most prominent feature of the '46 Chryslers was the "harmonica" grille and the unusual central overrider fitted to the front bumper. A less obvious innovation perhaps, although more significant in styling terms, is the manner in which the line of the front fenders was extended back into the doors, thereby achieving an altogether more updated look for an old body design. In this respect, at least, Chrysler were ahead of most of their rivals.

While the ash framework stayed throughout the Town & Country convertible's early life, the use of genuine mahogany for the insert panels was quickly dropped to save money. In 1947, Chrysler adopted Di-Noc decals but these were such good quality it was hard to distinguish them from the original wooden panels. The convertible Town & Country disappeared with the 1950 model, to be replaced by a hardtop coupe. From then on the name was applied to station wagons, until the idea of a wood-bodied ragtop was resurrected with the 1984 LeBaron Town & Country.

The 1946 Chrysler Town & Country is a prime example of how a truly classic design can evolve, almost by accident. It started out as an idea for a practical wagon with style, and turned into a beautiful car (particularly in open-top form) that was unfortunately short-lived in its original form. Would it have happened that way without the interruption of the Second World War? We will never know.

Above: As was the norm, 1946 Oldsmobiles were updated prewar models. The 4-door sedan was the most popular of the Custom Cruiser 98 series, selling 11,031.

Below: Looking cute wasn't enough for the Crosley to survive. This tiny car was in many ways out of place in a Cadillac-hungry society and by 1952 the marque was no more.

1947

The US auto industry lost two giants in 1947, William C. "Billy" Durant died on March 18 and Henry Ford on April 7. Both were founders of huge corporations, but only Ford and his family were to benefit. Durant wound up nearly broke and, in an attempt to spare the 4 million ex-servicemen returning to civilian life the same fate, the G.I. Bill was introduced.

"First by far with a postwar car" was Studebaker's proud boast when their 1947 models were introduced in April 1946. And there's no disputing the fact that the design, generally credited to Raymond Loewy, represented a major leap forward in automobile styling with the front fenders flush with the body. In fact, Studebaker were beaten into announcing their radical new models by the fledgling Kaiser-Frazer company who also brought out a slab-sided car (designed by Howard "Dutch" Darrin) in January. However, the Kaiser-Frazer

Right: Studebaker advertising carried the message "First by far with a postwar car!" and it would take the other major Detroit manufacturers a couple of years to catch up with the new designs from South Bend, Indiana.

First by far with a postwar car!

THE NEW 1947 STUDEBAKER

Built by America's finest automotive craftsmen

THEY'RE LOW!   THEY'RE LONG!   THEY'RE LUXURIOUS!

Below: The Commander Regal DeLuxe five-passenger Starlight Coupe was one of the top line Studebakers for '47. Most distinctive was the slab-sided front fenders integral with its main body.

offering was plainer and lacked the creative innovation of the products from South Bend, Indiana. And, if Studebaker was miffed at being upstaged in this way, at least their new cars went into production in May and were available to the public in June, well before the first Kaiser-Frazer cars hit the road in October.

Studebaker achieved a two to three year styling lead over the "Big Three" – primarily because of their use of an outside design studio rather than having company stylists and draughtsmen tied up with military work during the war. However, the story behind the new design is far from straightforward. Raymond Loewy Studios were the consultants, and establishing the advanced lines began in 1942 with the design team headed by Virgil Exner and Robert Bourke and assisted by clay modeler Frank Ahlroth. Loewy would make regular visits to the factory from New York to check on progress, but it seems his flamboyant personality upset some of the factory management – in particular Roy Cole, engineering vice president.

Virgil Exner also resented Loewy for taking the lion's share of the credit for design work he felt was his. So when he was approached by Cole early in 1944 to start a rival design project at home, in direct competition to his work for Loewy, Exner barely hesitated. To ensure that the Loewy design would fail to be accepted by Studebaker management, Cole deliberately gave Bob Bourke false dimensions for the car, resulting in a full-size mock-up being prepared which was both shorter and narrower than required.

Consequently, when the Loewy proposal was rejected for looking out of proportion, Cole was able to unveil Exner's effort for com-

Above: The rear styling of Studebakers gave rise to comments about it being difficult to tell which way the car was going, and you can see why. The difference between the rear window configurations: the wrap-around on the Starlight coupe (center) and ordinary coupe and sedan can easily be seen.

parison and it easily won the approval of the Studebaker hierarchy. Despite a desperate attempt by Loewy's team to re-size their design in just seven days, Cole had already put the production tooling in hand for the Exner model. As can be imagined, Raymond Loewy was outraged and immediately fired Exner, who was at once taken on by Cole to continue his design work for the company.

Therefore, it is not easy to attribute the design precisely. Although Exner is acknowledged as stipulating the flashier, more upright front end, it was very much a team effort. By the end of the war, there were 39 Loewy people working at the factory on styling and design, including noted designers: Gordon Buehrig, John Reinhart, Bob Koto, John Cuccio, Ted Brennan, Vince Gardner and Jack Aldrich – all of whom made a contribution.

Exner and Cole may have undermined Raymond Loewy's personal influence at Studebaker, but the overall design had been developed by his group under his guidance for several years, and many of his team continued to work on the cars. For example, Vince Gardner was responsible for detailing the '47 front grille, and John Reinhart designed the dashboard.

The 1947 Studebaker's most obvious styling feature – the wrap-around rear window and steeply sloping trunk – is found in its most extreme form on the Starlight coupe, but is equally prominent on the sedan models. This gave rise to jokes about how difficult it was to tell which way the car was going but, for Studebaker, it was heading in the right direction and the company moved to eighth place in the sales charts for '47, overtaking Oldsmobile for the seventh spot in '48.

Studebaker were not the first to use a one-piece, curved windshield, but the extensive glass certainly provided outstanding all-round visibility. "Wide Vision" was an apt name for the windshield and, combined with the split rear windows, it gave an unrivaled feel of light and space to the interiors. In fact, the insides of the '47 models were more spacious than their predecessors – up to 11 inches more hip room for example – although the overall height had dropped by four inches in line with the trend for longer and lower cars.

The dashboard looked ultra-modern with three round dials grouped together and framed by the steering wheel; most other manufacturers would continue to position the clock on the passenger side for some years in order to achieve a symmetrical layout. Another innovation was the use of back light illumination for the instruments to cut out glare; a method pioneered on aircraft during the war. Otherwise, the upholstery and trim

Above: The Sportsman convertible woodie was an attractive variation of the Ford ragtop but, at around $500 dearer than the all-steel convertible, only 2,274 were sold in '47. The body design was much the same as the '42 models with a face-lifted grille. The Sportsman was dropped after '48.

Right: The Pontiac Streamliner Sedan Coupe was typical of the carry-over models produced in immediate post war years by most manufacturers. The sweeping fastback style (called "Sport Dynamic" by Pontiac) was on the way out, as it restricted rear vision, passenger headroom and trunk space. Although reliable and competitively priced, Pontiac models were generally regarded as rather old-fashioned and were aimed at middle-aged buyers as opposed to the young.

was unremarkable and Loewy expressed his concern at the contrast between the new exterior styling and the old-fashioned interior. Studebaker would not budge, claiming that a lot of their customers were old retired people and wouldn't accept brightly-colored interiors.

While the Commander series of models at the top end of the Studebaker catalog rode on a 119 inch wheelbase (the Land Cruiser 4-door sedan was stretched a further four inches to give generous leg room to rear seat passengers), it was the smaller Champion series (112 inch wheelbase) that proved to be the most popular. Indeed, Raymond Loewy claimed he was the first man in the industry to use the term "compact car" when describing the Studebaker Champion.

Where the body shell and chassis engineering bristled with new ideas, the engine definitely did not. Although new powerplants had been researched and even a V12 considered, at the end of the day, a practical, cost-effective updated version of the flathead six cylinder from prewar models was settled upon. Champion models used a 169.6 cu.in. 80 horsepower version, while the larger Commanders had a 226.2 cu.in., 94hp engine. Transmission was a three-speed manual across the board, with a column gear shift, and an optional automatic overdrive. An interesting device was the Automatic Hill Holder (introduced on the 1936 Studebaker President)

which operated the brakes when the clutch pedal was depressed and prevented the car from rolling backwards.

The new 1947 Studebakers received complimentary media reaction. Motor Manual stating: "This is indeed tomorrow's car today!" It might not have quite been tomorrow's car, but it was sufficiently advanced that the design remained virtually unchanged until 1950, when Loewy (getting his own back on Exner) won the redesign contest with his famous "bullet-nose" creation. It wasn't until the 1953 model that the final traces of the '47 design were eliminated and, even then, it didn't look that dated, proving just how futuristic the original concept had been.

Above: Another model coming to the end of its life was the wooden-bodied station wagon. Buick was the last company to produce a true wooden wagon in '53, but this '47 shows how wood cladding had replaced a structural feature on the sides, although the rear door remained an all-timber construction.

1948

Americans had plenty to celebrate in 1948. The country was getting back on its feet after the war and life was returning to normal. To top it all, US athletes picked up no less than 38 gold medals at the Olympics held in London, England. It was also election year and there was a new President in The White House – Harry S. Truman. Later in the year, Truman was to sign the Marshall Plan, guaranteeing $6 billion for overseas aid. Some of that aid would be needed in Berlin, Germany, which was being blockaded by Soviet forces in one of the first moves of what would become the Cold War. Berlin was deep in the Soviet-occupied area of Germany, but the city itself had been split into zones administered by the Americans, British, French and Soviets. To keep their zones of the city alive, the Allies organized a massive, round-the-clock airlift, which kept the inhabitants supplied with all the essentials for daily life.

Back in the States, residents of San Bernadino, California, saw history in the making, as the first McDonald's hamburger stand opened. From this small beginning would grow first a nationwide chain of restaurants, then a world-wide chain that eventually would even penetrate the Soviet Union.

Fast food was not the only area of advance in 1948. The development of the transistor at the Bell Laboratories would soon lead to a burgeoning electronics industry, while the latest development in photography was the Polaroid camera.

In Detroit, the auto manufacturers were also making strides forward. In the years immediately after WW2, they had simply dusted off their pre-war designs, made a few cosmetic changes, then built them as fast as they could to satisfy the demands of a car-hungry public. Buyers did not mind that the designs were four or more years old; after years of not being able to buy a new car, anything with wheels would do. Besides, they simply had no choice; it was the only way for companies to pick up the reins of business after years of wartime production.

By 1948, however, new models were beginning to appear, often resulting from development work carried out in secret during the war, and utilizing techniques of manufacture founded in the war work. Experience gained in the manufacture of non-automotive products, particularly aircraft and aircraft components, opened the eyes of designers and engineers to new possibilities in automobile design and construction.

Hudson was one manufacturer that offered a new car for 1948 which was a real winner and, in some respects, unique compared to the rest of Detroit's offerings that year. It was known as the Step-down Hudson.

The new Hudson was based on a unibody design which, although not a new idea for an American car (Nash and Lincoln had already produced unibody designs), it was an innovative move at that time. As utilized in the Step-down design, the unibody arrangement gave greater passenger comfort and safety, together with a sleek, attractive appearance. However, there were pros and cons to this construction. Without the heavy chassis, a much lighter structure could be built saving both materials and cost. On the negative side, it was both difficult and expensive to make alterations to the design. This meant that the substantial changes in appearance, which had become an annual ritual in Detroit, were

Left: One of the most striking aspects of the Step-down Hudson was its height. The lowered floor provided a low seating position and, hence, a low roofline, emphasizing the sleekness of the design. This was accentuated by the close-fitting, wrap-around bumpers.

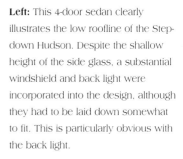

Left: This 4-door sedan clearly illustrates the low roofline of the Step-down Hudson. Despite the shallow height of the side glass, a substantial windshield and back light were incorporated into the design, although they had to be laid down somewhat to fit. This is particularly obvious with the back light.

Left: The unibody design incorporated box-section stiffeners to strengthen the structure and support the engine, transmission and suspension. A unique feature was the arrangement of the perimeter rails, which passed outside the rear wheels. Convertibles were made by sawing off the roof of club coupes and adding extra stiffeners under the floor, to the sides and around the opening of the passenger compartment.

out of the question. This would prove to be a major problem with the Step-down Hudson but, in 1948, the rapturous reception afforded the car outweighed doubts about the future.

Based on a 124 inch wheelbase, the body was designed to incorporate box-section stiffeners, which effectively formed a strong cage around the passenger compartment and provided support for the engine, transmission and suspension. These formed perimeter rails that ran under the doors and outside the rear wheels keeping intrusion into the passenger compartment to a minimum.

The "Step-down" name referred to the design of the passenger compartment itself. Aware that a low center of gravity would improve the car's handling and ride quality, Hudson designers arranged for the floor to be level with the bottom of the main perimeter rails, rather than sitting on top, which was normal practice with a separate chassis. To get into the car, it was necessary to step over the side rails and down onto the floor.

With a lower floor, it was possible to lower the position of the seats within the body and, consequently, the roofline while retaining good headroom inside. At 60 inches high, the new Hudson was four to six inches lower than most of its competitors, yet it provided as much, if not more, headroom. At the same time, ground clearance was not compromised. A two-piece driveshaft allowed the central floor hump to be quite low, improving comfort for passengers sitting in the middle of the seats.

Hudson engineers also improved the ride for passengers by cradling them between the axles, rather than having them sit over the axle at the rear, so the rear seat was positioned ahead of the axle. This allowed for a wider seat without requiring a wider body. Further elbow room was provided by arranging for the side glass to drop into the doors at an outward angle, allowing recesses to be formed in the door trim panels.

Although the roofline was lowered, the beltline was of conventional height, making the side glass quite shallow in depth – the bottom edge of the glass was level with passengers' shoulders. However, the windshield and back light were comparable in area to taller cars, although these were canted somewhat.

Power for the Step-down Hudson came from a choice of six or eight cylinder in-line engines. The former was a new powerplant – the Super Six, which had a capacity of 270 cu.in and developed 121 horsepower, while the latter was Hudson's tested Super Eight, a 254 cu.in. engine of 128 horsepower. Among the transmission options offered was overdrive, Drive-master and Vacumotive Drive, which had been available on previous mod-

els. Drivemaster was a form of automatic transmission, while the Vacumotive Drive gave automatic operation of the clutch alone.

The suspension was conventional coil-sprung independent at the front with parallel leaf springs at the rear. However, a heavy front stabilizer bar and rear panhard rod were incorporated to assist handling and ride.

A wide range of models was offered in the Super and Commodore series, comprising of 4-door sedans, 2-door broughams, club and standard coupes and convertible broughams.

When the Step-down was shown to Hudson dealers late in 1947, they could not believe their eyes. Worried about how long they could continue selling outdated pre-war designs in the face of steadily rising competition, they found the long, low and sleek automobile everything they could have wished for, and more. It was well received by road testers, too, who praised its styling, "roadability" and its comfort. For the next three years, the new Hudson would boost the small independent company's profits tremendously as the public stepped up to step down.

Top and above: The Tucker Torpedo was the brainchild of Preston Tucker, who had made a fortune during WW2 from the design of a gun turret mounting used in bomber aircraft. Fascinated by automobiles, after the war he set out to develop a car that would offer advanced engineering, styling, performance and levels of passenger safety. Powered by a 355 cu.in. rear-mounted, air-cooled, aluminum flat-six, the Torpedo could reach 60mph in 10 seconds and had a top speed of 120mph. For safety, its interior featured a padded dashboard and seatbelts, while a central third head-light turned with the steering so that the driver could see around corners at night. Sadly, Tucker's enterprise failed with accusations of fraud and dirty tricks played by Detroit's "Big Three" automobile makers. Only 50 examples of the futuristic Torpedo were completed.

Above: Cadillac's new model for 1948 was to set a styling trend that would become a prominent part of all Cadillac designs throughout the Fifties and be copied by most other manufacturers. The '48 Caddy was the first of many to feature tail fins. The car's designer, Franklin Q. Hershey, had developed the idea after seeing the Lockheed P38 Lightning airplane prior to WW2.

Left: The Frazer first appeared in 1947 and featured a high level of interior appointments in addition to its advanced, slab-sided styling with integral fenders. Built by Kaiser-Frazer, it outsold the products of the other independent auto makers until 1949, when co-founder Joe Frazer left the company. Although the company continued under the Kaiser name, never again would it enjoy the profits of that brief post-war period.

1949

The Berlin airlift came to an end and, still in the sky, James Gallagher made the first non-stop flight around the world in a Boeing B-50A Lucky Lady II, while another Boeing, the Stratocruiser, introduced new standards of airline passenger luxury. On the ground, more than 6 million cars poured out of factories and aviation influences abounded in the designs.

There was a momentous transformation in Ford's fortunes as their output nearly tripled and they zoomed into the number one spot, overtaking arch rivals Chevrolet. On the face of it, this tremendous success can be attributed to the brand new automobiles they had to offer, but there's more to it than that.

For a start, the 1949 model year spanned almost eighteen months, as the restyled cars were launched in June 1948 and remained on sale right up until November 1949. This early announcement also shortened the '48 model year considerably and reduced sales of the pre-war designs on offer in that year, which were much the same as the '46 and '47 Fords.

Even taking all this into account, it has to be said that the '49 Ford was worthy of all the media attention and phenomenal sales that followed. The Ford is significant because it was the first low-price car with a slab-sided body devoid of any of the traditional fender lines. Other makes such as Hudson (another landmark in automobile styling), Nash and Kaiser-Frazer also produced similar concepts but they were not as successful nor as cheap as the Ford. Chevrolet and Plymouth, meanwhile, still had pronounced rear fenders and an obvious dip between head lights and hood.

In fact, the slab-sided Fords were regarded as so flat that they soon earned the nickname "shoeboxes", though today it's hard to equate the curved lines with a shoebox. Engineering was revolutionary too (for a Ford!); this was the beginning of exciting times for the blue oval brigade. Following the death of founder Henry Ford in 1947, his grandson Henry Ford II introduced swinging changes and sought to rid the company of old-fashioned practices.

One of young Henry's most stalwart supporters was executive vice president Ernest Breech, and it is chiefly due to his efforts that the company won through. Breech also had a significant effect on the styling of the '49 Ford models, as we shall see later on. But the first things to disappear were the transverse leaf springs and beam axle suspension that old

Above: Ford advertising vigorously suggested "There's a New Ford in your future" and highlighted its "Mid Ship" ride and "Sofa-Wide" seats which attracted over a million customers.

Left: Despite a higher price tag, the 1949 Ford Custom Club Coupe proved itself to be a more popular choice than the standard version. Evidently most people weren't bothered about the possible saving of $96, and 150,254 Custom coupes were produced against only 4,170 of the cheaper ones. The extra money gave you such essentials as chrome window trims instead of rubber, a horn ring on the steering wheel, twin sun visors, dual arm rests and a chrome strip along the body sides.

THE AMERICAN AUTOMOBILE

Right: The new Rocket overhead valve 303 cu.in. V8 engine was a hot performer and, consequently, an Oldsmobile 88 convertible made a good choice as the pace car for the 1949 Indianapolis 500. Here an Olds 98 convertible (not the official pace car) is posed alongside one of the legendary Novi-engined race cars, the Mobil Special Kurtis roadster.

Below: Nash brought out radical Airflyte-styled cars in 1949, soon to be dubbed "bathtubs". The unitary construction (without separate body and chassis) was a first for a mass production US manufacturer. Nash claimed the shape produced 20% less drag, but under those curves lurked an old-fashioned in-line six. "There's Much of Tomorrow In All Nash Does Today" ran the slogans. Nash was replaced by Rambler in 1958.

Above: For his inauguration on January 20th, President Harry S. Truman rode to the ceremony in style in a Lincoln Cosmopolitan convertible. Totally restyled for '49 with a modern streamlined appearance, prestige, luxury and distinction were all attributes that Lincoln promised its owners saying "you may drive it everywhere with pride". Recessed headlights and wide chrome grille helped differentiate the bigger Cosmopolitan from similar-shaped Mercury models (some Mercury body panels were shared with the smaller Lincoln EL series), but all Lincolns also had a new 336 cu.in. V8 for improved performance.

Henry insisted upon, to be replaced with coil spring independent front and longitudinal leaf rear suspension. Gone too, was the two-speed rear axle and in its place optional overdrive.

The engine was moved five inches forward to create a lower profile, yet provide greater internal space within a slightly shorter and narrower body. This allowed more leg room for the people in the front seat, and with the rear seat now positioned ahead of the rear axle (instead of between the wheels), an extra six inches of width for the passengers in the back. Advertising emphasized this additional comfort by describing the seats as "Sofa-Wide" and promoting the "Mid Ship Ride" and Hydra-Coil front springs. The new Ford design also created 57% more trunk space, now denoted as a "Deep Deck Luggage Locker". And if that wasn't enough, then surely the Magic Air temperature control system, Magic Action brakes or Picture Window visibility would do the trick?

It's estimated that around 28 million people visited the dealers' showrooms in the first three days after the new models were announced. What drew them were attractive cars that had progressed from initial design to production in just 19 months (in those days, average lead times were about three years). Haste wasn't without its problems, of course, and the build quality on the first '49s wasn't as good as it might have been. Body rattles

plagued early vehicles and a number of alterations were made to alleviate problems. This situation persisted throughout the '49 model run and wasn't fully resolved until the 1950 models came along. But it didn't stop the '49 Ford becoming a huge hit and the company outsold Chevrolet by a large margin, with 1.1 million cars coming off the assembly lines.

Indeed, the success of the 1949 models is often credited for saving Ford from oblivion – it really was that desperate. Whether an organization of such magnitude would have disappeared completely is open to conjecture but this automobile has warranted a special place in Ford's long and varied history.

The genesis of such a ground-breaking model was not without complications and there have been many claims as to how the design came about. The first stage in the saga began when Ford's head designer, Eugene T. "Bob" Gregorie showed his ideas to Ernest Breech in 1946. Breech liked the proposal, but felt it was too big to be marketed as a Ford, and in September '46 he pronounced that Gregorie's prototype would instead be used for the more upmarket Mercury range.

This naturally left a big hole in the planning process, and Gregorie immediately started work preparing an alternative design for the Ford. At the same time Breech contracted his friend George Walker (who operated a design consultancy that had done a lot of work for Nash) to come up with some ideas. On the staff were Elwood Engel, Joseph Oros, Richard Caleal, Holden Koto and Bob Bourke. When it came time to make the presentation, Gregorie submitted one clay model and the Walker studio put up three for consideration.

Although there seems to have been very little to choose between them, Breech picked one of Walker's designs. Gregorie left Ford a short time later although they remained on friendly terms. Walker's team proceeded to develop the design and developed the spinner in the center of the grille. Precisely who thought up this idea is debatable. Until recently it was accepted that the front end of the '49 Ford was the work of Caleal, Bourke and Koto – the latter two either working directly for Walker, or moonlighting from the Loewy studio (and the '50 Studebaker with its similar spinner was definitely a Bourke creation for Loewy). However, Oros has stated emphatically that the spinner was his creation.

Whatever the truth, it is apparent that there were many influences during what must have been a hectic period. George Walker took most of the credit at the time and used it to good effect to promote his agency, but it was Ernest Breech and Henry Ford II who had the final say on what went into production.

1950

The dark clouds of war gathered again as US troops were sent to South Korea to help fight off the invasion from the north, and President Truman declared a state of emergency. Another rather sinister spectacle, closer to home, was the communist witch hunt conducted by Senator Joe McCarthy, but Boston University president Daniel Marsh was more concerned with television turning 150 million Americans into "a nation of morons".

Sometimes, the hardest task for a designer is altering a car to make it look different from last year's model. Occasionally this results in a classic, but mostly it looks exactly what it really is – a face-lifted version of the earlier car.

Annual changes put pressure on stylists to produce alterations significant enough for the customers to know this was a new car, yet without making fundamental modifications to the structure. Cost restrictions meant that the body sheet metal and major engineering components were used for at least three years, so often a designer was restricted to reworking the front end, the body moldings and fancying-up the rear. The chance to re-design the car every year wouldn't come until later.

Faced with "improving" their elegant 1949 creations, staff at the GM Art & Color Studio, who had responsibility for Buick, decided a bold statement was required – and they don't come much bolder than the buck-toothed grille! While overall responsibility was Harley Earl's, pin-pointing which designer should take the credit (if credit's the right word) for the row of exaggerated bumper guards is not easy. Various people have laid claim, but as most of them are now dead, it's probably impossible to give a definitive answer.

We do know that Ned Nickles, Harlow "Red" Curtice, Edward T. Ragsdale and Henry Lauve were involved. Nickles and Lauve worked under Earl, Curtice had been Buick general manager until 1948 when he was promoted and Ragsdale was manufacturing manager. Nickles is regarded as the leading Buick stylist at that time and is acknowledged for contributing such features as the VentiPorts and sweepspear side decorations. Lauve claimed the dummy porthole VentiPorts and the "Toothy Wonder" grille were his idea.

There seems no dispute as to who was involved with introducing the hardtop body style – Nickles, Ragsdale and Curtice – although, yet again, details of precisely how

Above: There was no mistaking a Buick in 1950! No other car could match those chrome teeth filling a gaping grille. Behind the Roadmaster's bucktooth smile was a trusted 320 cu.in. straight eight engine and Buick's own Dynaflow automatic transmission. Note the four elongated VentiPorts.

Left: Chrome "sweepspear" decoration on the body sides was another Buick trademark. The Roadmaster convertible was the most expensive model (apart from a limited production station wagon) at almost $3,000 and sold in correspondingly low numbers. Other Buicks were more sought-after, though, and model year production rose to around 670,000 cars.

Above: The 1950 Chevrolet DeLuxe
Fleetline 4-door sedan is virtually
identical to the first proper post-war
designs introduced a year earlier. The
beginnings of Fifties styling
flamboyance are evident, together
with the increasing use of chrome,
even on lower-price cars, but the
sleek fastback shape was soon to go
out of fashion as restricted rear vision
was a problem. The brand new two-
speed Powerglide automatic was a
Chevy breakthrough at the cheaper
end of the market, but the ancient
Stovebolt six was still the only engine
available.

Above right: The Studebaker Starlight
Coupe was about as original as a
design could get. The large chrome
spinner in the center of the grille has
obvious aircraft connotations and the
wrap-around rear window was
another unusual feature. Although
regarded today purely as a classic
example of innovative styling, the
controversial shape created huge
public interest and the company
enjoyed its best year ever.

it came about are far from conclusive. The
concept dates from 1945 and, depending on
who you believe, either Nickles or Ragsdale
came up with the suggestion of a body style
that looked like a convertible but had a steel
roof. The most quoted source of inspiration is
Ragsdale's wife, Sarah, who liked convertible
models for their looks but didn't enjoy driving
them with the top down because her hair got
blown around. Nickles believed that Ragsdale
saw a model of his and took up the idea.

The role played by Curtice was pivotal.
Although no longer officially involved in the
day-to-day running of Buick, he remained
very much in charge, dominating easy-going
general manager Ivan L. Wiles who had taken
over his position. The idea of a huge division
like Buick being treated as a personal fiefdom

might seem incredible today, but Red Curtice
held a unique position, having taken the marque from the depths of depression, through
the traumas of war and into the boom years
of the Fifties. So it was Curtice, either working
directly or by pressurizing people behind the
scenes, who directed how Buick progressed.

And progress Buick certainly did. While it
is easy to fault the amount of chrome used or
the bizarre aspects of the design, in its day
the voluptuous Buick was a highly-regarded
automobile, only one step down from a
Cadillac, and to be behind the wheel of Buick
was a sign of a successful career. Forecasting
the growth of the automobile market, in 1945
Curtice had persuaded General Motors' chief
executive Alfred P. Sloan to fund an expan-
sion programme to increase Buick's manufac-

turing capacity to over half a million vehicles a year. It was a couple of years before that total was reached, but 1950 saw it exceeded by a wide margin and Buick leapt to number three in the sales charts, behind Chevrolet and Ford – a remarkable achievement.

The curvaceous nature of the Buick was accentuated by a body line that sloped down from the top of the headlight and dipped in front of the rear wheel before climbing back up and giving a distinct definition to the rear fender. This was at a period when most other body styles tried to eliminate the rear fender shape and harks back to Harley Earl's 1939 Y-Job Buick concept car which foretold many of the styling ingredients that were to become identified with Buick in the 1950s.

One of the smallest of these styling arti-facts was the gunsight or bombsight hood ornament. Back in 1946, Nickles produced a design that would be suitable for mass pro-duction, based on the Y-Job ornament, and the feature remained until 1958. Undoubtedly more of a Buick trademark were the VentiPorts on the sides of the front fenders. Nickles is almost always credited for these (copied from a fighter plane exhaust stubs) when he cut holes in the hood of his '48 Roadmaster con-vertible and fixed lights behind them wired to the distributor so they would flash like exhausts.

Ragsdale was horrified at seeing Nickles' customizing and complained to Curtice that the young designer had ruined a perfectly good car. Curtice looked for himself and, far

from censuring Nickles, incorporated the port-holes in the 1949 Buick models. Initially these VentiPorts were said to release fumes from the engine compartment and were fully func-tional. For various reasons – not least reports of inebriated passers-by using the orifices to urinate on the engine – the holes were blanked off and they became purely decorative. For 1950 models, the VentiPorts were elongated to look like slots; the more expensive models had four per side, while others had three.

The excess chrome on postwar Buicks was explained by Nickles as coming about due to a shortage during the war. Once free of restrictions, designers used chrome for glam-or and perhaps overdosed on the shiny stuff. Nickles was quoted as saying: "...we were entertaining people with chrome on cars..." and it surely did that. Not all designers took such a sanguine attitude in later years, Henry Lauve calling it 'Club Sandwich Chrome' and you can see what he means. Lauve also said that the huge teeth only came about because "...we wanted to be different..." Again, there can be little argument that they succeeded!

However, looking at the era in which the 1950 Buicks were conceived, they were total-ly appropriate for their time. Big, bold, brash, certainly – yet they established keynote fea-tures that would instantly tell you that the car was a Buick from a block or more away, not something that can be done that easily in the Nineties. Stylish? Yes, the 1950 Buick had style aplenty and it showed.

Left: The Pontiac Chieftain convertible was another General Motors product that only had limited revisions from the previous year, although the massive grille seems fairly restrained when compared to that of the Buick. The characteristic Silver Streak styling of chrome strips running back over the hood had been around since the Thirties and the Indian Head ornament (which lit up at night) remained as a fixture until 1957. This car has the 268 cu.in. straight eight L-head engine, but in-line six cylinder powerplants were also available.

1951

The war in Korea was dragging on, although the US Army was on the offensive and had recaptured Seoul, and it came as something of a shock when president Harry S. Truman sacked General Douglas MacArthur for defying the civil authority in April. Further shocks were felt when an atomic bomb was tested in Nevada, just 45 miles from Las Vegas, and the first hydrogen bomb was detonated on an atoll in the Marshall Islands, in the Pacific Ocean. But probably the biggest explosion in America was the increasing television audience which had risen to 9% of all homes and continued to escalate at an ever faster rate.

Truce finally came to Korea in November, and things became easier for some drivers who chose to buy a Chrysler with the auto industry's first viable power steering system, called "Hydraguide". At the lower end of the market, three-speed automatic transmissions could now be had on Ford and Mercury cars – the Ford-O-Matic and Merc-O-Matic units, built in conjunction with Warner Gear – but it was something of an exaggeration for Mercury to advertise its '51 models using the slogan "Nothing like it on the road!"

The Mercury nameplate suffered from something of an identity crisis – it was usually looked upon as a fancy Ford rather than a junior Lincoln. The 1951 models (the last of a three year phase starting with the '49 designs) were more Lincoln in appearance, although beneath the bodywork there were mostly Ford mechanical parts.

In an attempt to give Mercury automobiles a more upmarket image, the Lincoln-Mercury division was formed in October 1945. This also gave Lincoln an independent dealership network whereas its cars had previously been sold in selected Ford showrooms.

As we know from the story behind the creation of the 1949 Ford models, it was Ernest Breech who decided that Bob Gregorie's initial design should be used for the Mercury range. But the development of the shape that was to become inextricably linked with the Fifties wasn't quite as straight-forward as simply changing the name on the hood.

In fact, the evolution of the 1951 Mercury involved three generations of the mighty Ford dynasty and, in some ways, encapsulated the end of the old autocratic regime that had grown up under the ailing Henry Ford and the new beginnings heralded with the arrival of

Left: According to the advertisement copy writers, there was nothing like a '51 Mercury on the road, but its striking similarity to the models of the previous two years was unmissable.

Below: There were few major changes to the Mercury '51. The 4-door sedan was the top seller and one third of the buyers opted for Merc-O-Matic automatic transmission.

THE AMERICAN AUTOMOBILE

Right: Totally redesigned by John Reinhart, the 24th Series Packards for '51 were acclaimed as "the most beautiful car of the year" by the Society of Motion Picture Art Directors. The line up consisted of three main levels of models – the lower priced 200 (back) had a "toothless" grille with a 288 cu.in. engine and 122 inch wheelbase; the mid-range 300 (center) had a 5 inch longer wheelbase and bigger engine; the top of the line 400 Patrician (front) only came as a 4-door sedan.

Below: The Packard 250 convertible was a mid-year introduction, together with a companion 2-door Hardtop coupe. It was based on the shorter wheelbase of the 200 series, but used the larger 327 cu.in. in-line eight cylinder L-head engine. Four dummy louvers on the rear fenders and fancy interiors featured in these models.

his grandson, Henry Ford II. Gregorie first started work on the design when Edsel Ford was in charge of styling and, although the two shared many ideas, they were by no means in total agreement. Edsel Ford tended to favor a lighter touch, especially on details like bumpers and grille, whereas Gregorie was more inclined to use broader brush strokes.

The death of Edsel Ford on May 26 1943 was a turning point. Grief-stricken at the loss, Octogenarian Henry took even less interest in the cars bearing his name, and left important decisions to others – mainly Harry Bennett and Charlie Sorensen – as the battle waged for control of the Ford empire. Vice-president, "Cast Iron Charlie" Sorensen saw the Gregorie proposals and encouraged the stylist to make the cars even bigger and more rounded, equating size and luxury to the voluptuous curves of "those big Italian gals".

But Sorensen was part of the old guard and on his way out, eventually to be deposed early in 1944. However, the internal power struggle wouldn't be fully resolved until some time after Henry Ford II became company president in September 1945. Young Henry hired new management to replace Bennett and his cronies and, in one of his most crucial appointments, was to take on a group of ten young ex-USAAF officers headed by Charles "Tex" Thornton, who quickly became known as "The Whizz Kids" throughout Ford. Ernest Breech was then persuaded to join the company and things really started to happen.

One effect was a rationalization of the Ford, Mercury and Lincoln models. It was decided that Mercurys would use a 118 inch wheelbase chassis (required for the larger body shell shared with Lincoln) of similar dimensions to pre-war designs although completely new in concept, while Fords would sit on a four inch shorter platform. Meantime, Lincoln used two slightly longer configurations – 121 and 125 inches – as befitted their status as a luxury marque.

Although Bob Gregorie had left Ford in 1946, his design for the 1949 Mercury went into production with very little modification. Subsequent face-lifts in '50 and '51 improved the overall look, adding extended rear fenders and vertical tail lights. The bodywork may have altered little, but a brand new feature on the 1951 was of more significance to the buyer – the Merc-O-Matic automatic transmission.

Coupled to an outmoded Flathead V8, the automatic put the Mercury's performance into the "leisurely" bracket or, as Mechanix

Illustrated tester Tom McCahill put it: "...the winged Mercury parked his track shoes outside the door and joined the ladies over a comforting pot of tea". Mercury adverts highlighted economy, promising to "Squeeze the last mile out of a gallon", and stressed that it wasn't expensive either, saying they gave customers "more car per dollar". The hot rodders' favorite had been turned into something different, something more comforting to Mr and Mrs Joe Average – for it was they who were buying new automobiles. The difference appealed and, with sales over 310,000, raised Mercury to number six in the charts.

But if the '51 Mercury was a success with the older generation when new, it would gain a far more long-lasting image as a Fifties icon from a most unlikely source – the death of a film star. Had he lived, it is impossible to predict what would have become of James Dean, but one thing is certain – he would never have driven a Mercury except in a movie. The fact that his second starring role in "A Rebel Without A Cause" (released in 1955 shortly after his fatal car crash) featured him as a super cool teenager fighting the establishment and driving a mildly customized Mercury was to endow the car with a presence that endures today.

The association with James Dean fixed the "bathtub" Mercury as an automobile with attitude – performance didn't matter, it was all about looking cool as you cruised to the drive-in. Over the years, Hollywood periodically reinforced this image, notably in the 1970s blockbuster "American Graffiti" in which the customized Mercury was used by a delinquent gang of youngsters.

From comfortable family transport for the suburban dweller to an everlasting symbol of teenage rebellion, surely no other car has made such a remarkable transition as the Mercury?

Below: Lee Wallard won the 1951 Indianapolis 500 in his Belanger Motors Special at an average speed of 126.244mph. This marked the 28th consecutive victory on Firestone tires at the Brickyard, and was proclaimed in adverts with the slogan "Safety-proved on the Speedway for your protection on the highway", stressing that 500 miles on the track equalled five years of average driving.

1952

Many US industrialists profited hugely from government contracts during the Second World War, and one of the most famous was Henry John Kaiser who had interests in ship-building and construction. Like other tycoons who made vast fortunes over the years, Kaiser thought he could take on the established Detroit auto makers and beat them at their own game. And, just like all "outside" attempts to launch a new postwar car, Kaiser's venture ended in failure.

Henry Kaiser's dream was a small, cheap car that would provide basic transportation for everyone. In the early 1940s, he had predicted producing a new car for $400 – a suggestion which proved to be totally unrealistic, yet one Kaiser often repeated in his quest for publicity. It was in an attempt to revive the flagging fortunes of his auto company, that he decided to launch the new small car in September 1950 and borrowed 44 million dollars to finance the tooling required.

Stylist Howard "Dutch" Darrin produced a prototype based on his 1951 full-size Kaiser design but, instead, Henry decided to go with another concept put together by American Metal Products of Detroit. Based on a 100 inch wheelbase chassis, the compact Henry J (as it came to be called) 2-door sedan was notable for its sloping fastback and small tail fins. The fins were part of Darrin's attempt to improve the looks of the car, and he made several other changes, including his trade-

Above: The small Henry J 2-door sedan was launched as an economy car that anyone could afford. Priced at $1664, the top of the line Corsair DeLuxe version came with glove box and opening trunk lid – items that came as standard on even the most basic cars. The 161 cu.in. six cylinder engine gave a 0-60mph time of 14 seconds. The central bar of the grille should be chrome, not painted.

Right: Outwardly, the 1951 and 1952 Chrysler models were identical, but under the hood of Saratoga and New Yorker models was the first legendary Hemi V8 – a 331 cu.in. overhead valve engine that produced 180bhp in standard form. The Windsor Highlander convertible only had a 119hp 264 cu.in. L-head in-line six cylinder engine and so was far more sedate.

Right: In an attempt to boost flagging sales in '52, Kaiser managed to persuade department store chain Sears Roebuck to market the car using their Allstate brand name. Little more than a Henry J with a different grille and interior, despite aggressive promotion, less than 1,600 Allstates were sold in 1952, and the scheme was dropped in '53 after fewer than 800 orders had been taken.

mark feature – a slight dip in the bodywork just behind the door. Power for the Henry J came from either a 68hp flathead Willys 134 cu.in. four cylinder engine or a 161 cu.in. six that gave 80 horsepower.

Initially it seemed as though Kaiser had come up with a winner as almost 82,000 Henry Js were sold in 1951. That seems to have saturated the market though, as sales more than halved in '52, then halved again in '53. In 1954, the car's last year, only 1,123 were sold and that was the end. Henry Kaiser's mistake was to believe that there was a huge market for a cheap car with no trimmings. He was quoted as saying, "We feel that we have accomplished our goal at a price which will be within the budgets of millions who have never been able to afford a new car." But Kaiser had failed to understand that most Americans in the early Fifties preferred to own a car that looked glitzy rather than one classed as "a poor man's automobile".

While Kaiser's aim was to produce a cheap, no-frills automobile, that didn't prevent copywriters from filling the company sales litera-ture with fulsome descriptions. Calling the mundane flathead engines "Supersonic" was par for the period, but stating that the feeble four cylinder "Lunges like a lion (without the roar!)", was definitely over the top! Other animal connotations were used, such as "Tough as an Ox, nimble as a Kitten" but, in an attempt to make the Henry J appeal to as wide an audience as possible, there were also statements like "You'll be the object of envy at the doors of the smartest shops".

The Henry J saw some international competition use too. Three cars were entered in the 1952 Monte Carlo Rally, and one actually finished in 20th place – an incredible achievement. But even had a Henry J won the event outright, it would not have been enough to stop Kaiser's dream becoming a nightmare.

Sales plummeted and debts mounted. Kaiser amalgamated with Willys-Overland in 1954, and the following year Kaiser-Willys ceased manufacture of passenger cars. Henry J. Kaiser's venture into the automobile world was estimated to have lost 100 million dollars in a decade.

1953

Ford and Buick shared 1953 as their Golden Anniversary Year and Charles E. Wilson, president of GM, made his famous (and often misquoted) statement: "...for many years I thought that what was good for our country was good for General Motors, and vice-versa". What eventually turned out good for Chevrolet was the arrival of a brand new sports car.

Whenever the reasons behind the birth of the Corvette are chronicled, it is usually suggested that it was GIs returning from Europe with an enthusiasm for British or Italian sports cars that led to the creation of America's favorite two-seater. While not wishing to diminish this idea, it is worth pointing out that, in 1952, little more than 11,000 new sports cars were registered across the entire USA – approximately 0.025% of the nation's new car market.

Given this perspective, it is easy to understand why the big Detroit automobile makers were not exactly fighting each other to enter such a small, specialized sector of the marketplace. That it should be Chevrolet – traditionally a purveyor of affordable, yet mundane, family sedans – to introduce such a

bold departure from the norm, is almost entirely due to the efforts of two men – Harley Earl and Ed Cole.

As the stylist supremo at General Motors, Harley Earl used his considerable influence to mount almost a personal crusade to prove that his company could build a car as good as the Jaguars and Ferraris he so admired. Chief engineer Cole, on the other hand, saw a sports car would boost the Chevrolet name and give it a more youthful image. In addition to the two major players, the names of Robert McLean and Maurice Olley should be added. Newly arrived from Cal Tech, when laying out the chassis design, young McLean decided to reverse the normal procedure and started at the back axle, then worked forward to obtain the 50:50 weight distribution specified. Most of the suspension and steering details came from Olley (an ex-Rolls Royce engineer) and their efforts helped give the Corvette its road-hugging profile, thanks to the lower slung engine and drivetrain.

Following the debut of the prototype EX-122 Corvette in the GM Motorama – a glamorous cavalcade of exotic cars that toured the USA throughout the Fifties – Chevrolet dealers found themselves inundated with enquiries about the sporty two-seater. It seemed Earl and Cole had produced a winning concept and the car was put into production without many alterations. This wasn't so easy. Using glass-fiber for a concept car was fine, but

adapting the design and building techniques for the assembly line was another matter.

Compromises were inevitable; the Chevy engineers and designers were further hampered because they were forced, in the most part, to use existing mechanical components to save time and keep the cost of the project down to a minimum. This meant that the Corvette came with a six cylinder Stovebolt engine and a Powerglide two-speed automatic transmission. Of course, Cole's team tweaked the old Chevy six to produce 150 horsepower and push the speedo needle round to almost 110mph, but it just wasn't in the same league as Jaguar's twin overhead camshaft powerplant.

Thomas Keating, Chevrolet's general manager, described the new two-seater thus: "In the Corvette we have built a sports car in the American tradition. It is not a racing car in the accepted sense that a European sports car is a race car. It is intended rather to satisfy the American public's conception of beauty, comfort and convenience, plus performance."

On 30th June 1953, the first ever Corvette (one of only 300 built in that year) was driven off the end of a short, six car-length assembly line tucked away in a corner of the Chevrolet

Above: The dramatic new Studebaker Commander Starliner hardtop was the most elegant of Raymond Loewy designs and won a Fashion Academy Award, but production difficulties held back sales.

Below: The DeSoto Firedome V8, with hemispherical combustion chambers on a 276 cu.in. engine, produced an impressive 160bhp.

plant in Flint, Michigan. Joining together the 46 separate glass-fiber panels that made up the body, getting them to cure and mounting it on the chassis was a labor-intensive task and, at times, the process was a slow and uncertain affair.

Because of the apparently huge demand and the shortage of cars, it was decided to allocate the available Corvettes to celebrities and prominent figures in the first instance. However, when the cars fell short of expectations, this method of selective distribution backfired and generated some rather unwelcome negative publicity. Only 183 Corvettes were sold in '53, and production had to be held in check the following year as manufacture was transferred to St Louis. It didn't help that, priced at $3490, the Corvette was over a thousand dollars more than an MG and out of reach of the majority of young drivers it was supposedly aimed at.

Despite Thomas Keating's pronouncement, comparisons between European sport cars and the Corvette were inevitable. And, not unexpectedly, the Chevy two-seater didn't stand up well against such competitors. It wasn't just the less-than-exciting six cylinder engine, or Powerglide automatic, but also the dashboard and whitewall tires that didn't belong on a sports car. And even those people prepared to accept the lack of performance were far from satisfied with the level of standard equipment – no external door handles, clumsy clip-in side curtains instead of wind-up windows, a primitive convertible top that let in rain and dust – and distressing rattles from the glass-fiber bodywork.

Most other automobile manufacturers would have swiftly abandoned such a troublesome project as this. The fact that a huge company like Chevrolet kept the sports car alive and that the Corvette itself survives to the present day comes back, once again, to the influence wielded by Harley Earl and Ed

Cole. Maybe some of it was simply a matter of pride and Earl protecting his reputation, unwilling to accept that his creation was, by most standards, a failure. Or perhaps Cole realized that when the new V8 engine arrived, Chevy would take on a whole new performance image – he certainly never lost his enthusiasm for the car.

In many ways the 1953 Corvette is an anachronism. At the time it was a car that Chevrolet should never have made. A giant company busy churning out 1.3 million family cars a year had no logical reason to undertake the construction of a tiny quantity of hand-built vehicles, using a curious combina-tion of special materials and stock compo-nents. But among many other facets of his character, Harley Earl was a dedicated car enthusiast and designing a sports car that would be internationally acclaimed obviously represented to him a challenge that he just couldn't resist.

His first attempt, while regarded as a Fifties classic today, fell woefully short of the type of car he wanted to emulate. But at least it was built and, in time, it would develop into a true sports car and one that Harley Earl, Ed Cole and all those Corvette designers and engineers that followed them could truly be proud of.

Above: A very special Buick was the Roadmaster Skylark Anniversary Convertible for 1953. Unique styling features included fenders with full round wheel openings, no VentiPorts in the hood, and sweepspear trim plus special body emblems. A lower roof line and 40-spoke Kelsey-Hayes wire wheels added to the opulent look, while the leather interior came as standard with a package of luxury accessories. At $5,000 the Skylark was the most expensive Buick and cost more than some Cadillacs; it's no wonder only 1,690 were produced.

1954

A ten year, $50 billion expansion program of the US highway system was announced by Vice-President Richard Nixon, and General Motors produced its 50 millionth car (a Chevrolet) on November 23rd at Flint, Michigan, which was paraded through the city streets in front of huge crowds.

Until the 1952 model year, the cars produced by Lincoln were aimed squarely at Cadillac customers and consequently designed for luxury motoring. Performance and road holding were of secondary consideration. This supposedly all changed when Earl S. MacPherson – vice president and chief engineer of Ford's Lincoln-Mercury Division – announced that, henceforth, the main target would be the Oldsmobile Ninety-Eight.

There was some sense in MacPherson's proposal as Lincoln had fared pretty badly against the outstanding 1949-51 Cadillacs, and the design team were given a strict brief to work to. However, excellent as the resulting car was, it wasn't quite the Oldsmobile equivalent that had been foreseen. Size-wise it came close – while the Lincoln had a one inch shorter wheelbase than the Olds 98, its overall length was an inch more. However, the Lincoln tipped the scales at nearly 400 pounds heavier – a weight definitely more in the Cadillac class. Under the Lincoln's hood, the new Y-block 317.5 cu.in. overhead valve V8's 160 horsepower rating was on a par with the smaller capacity Olds engine, but 30bhp down on the larger Cadillac powerplant.

Unfortunately, the '52 Lincolns were the subject of a massive 25% price hike over the previous year and, because of this, most Oldsmobile models would seem quite a bit cheaper by comparison. Therefore, in many respects, the Lincoln team were only partially successful in achieving their aims.

But bald dimensions and stark statistics can't possibly give you a feeling of what great cars the 1952-54 Lincolns really were. Gone was the bulbous carapace of an overblown Mercury body, and in its place was revealed a true "jet age" creation. And, not only did they look good, thanks to some splendid engineering the Lincoln was able to boast excellent performance, superior road holding and impressive reliability. When discussing their mechanical aspects, one recent commentator described them as "engineers' cars" – an apt appraisal.

Even so, over the years, many good automobiles have failed to sell in sufficient numbers. Fortunately for Lincoln, when it came to sales promotion they had two major advantages – the Carrera PanAmericana and Tom McCahill. That an automobile intended for upmarket American buyers could compete in, and win, the gruelling 1,900 mile Mexican

Below: The Lincoln Capri has been prepared as a replica of cars used in the Mexican Carrera PanAmericana road race back in the early '50s. The MacPherson suspension, strong chassis and highly efficient 317 cu.in. engine earned these Lincolns a reputation as performance machines.

cross-country road race was a truly remarkable feat, and thanks in no small part to the skilled preparation carried out by Bill Stroppe and wizard mechanic Clay Smith. Mind you, they had a good platform to work with, plus an ample factory supply of special "export" engine and suspension components – not forgetting some daredevil drivers!

In the 1952 event, Lincoln not only won the Stock Car Class, they also took 2nd, 3rd and 4th places. Winning driver Chuck Stevenson likened the experience to "riding a steel bridge across Mexico" when assessing the durability of the Lincoln chassis. A repeat performance followed in '53, with Lincoln again capturing the top four spots. 1954 also

Below: The clean front end design of the Lincoln was achieved by using the bumper as the central bar of the grille opening. Capri sales rose by 10% in 1954 to 29,500 and Hydra-Matic transmission (bought from arch rivals General Motors) was standard across the Lincoln range.

saw another Lincoln victory, although this time things weren't quite so straightforward. In fact, four of the factory-backed cars dropped out very early on and it was a private entrant who captured first place, although a surviving team car did take second place. Three wins in three years produced excellent publicity and Lincoln made good use of the successes.

Tom McCahill wasn't a race driver, but a well-respected writer who was responsible for road test reports in the immensely popular Mechanix Illustrated magazine and, consequently, a man of considerable influence. McCahill was a devoted fan of the 1952-54 Lincolns, even to the extent that he bought a '53 model for his own personal use! His review of the 1952 Lincoln could hardly have been more enthusiastic: "This is one of the finest handling big American cars I have ever driven...in the luxury and comfort departments I found it unbeatable...this car held the turns like a leech. It was a true pleasure to steer. This is undoubtedly one of the finest American cars ever built." It wasn't all praise, mind you, McCahill berating Ford for fitting too small an engine in the big car.

Two years later, McCahill was still enjoying the ride: "Last year I wrote that the 1953 Lincoln was America's finest and safest automobile. This still goes in 1954. These are magnificent road cars that will out-ride and

out-corner any other American car I have ever driven." He was happier about the engine too as that had been uprated to 205 horsepower. But the prime reason for McCahill's unstinting approval of the Lincoln's handling capability came from the new ball joint front suspension. This system did away with the traditional king pin arrangement, making the cars more stable at high speed (the Lincoln race cars could reach 130mph) and had been used before on some European cars.

The design of the Lincoln ball joint suspension (the forerunner of the suspension type currently used as standard equipment on cars around the world) was the result of a

Above: The futuristic fiber glass bodied Kaiser-Darrin two-seater sports car was designed by Howard "Dutch" Darrin using a Henry J chassis and 161 cu.in. Willys in-line six cylinder engine. Three-speed transmission with overdrive gave nearly 100mph top speed and 0-60mph could be done in 13 seconds. The car had unique sliding doors, and a folding top with an intermediate half-up position. Less than 500 were produced before the closure of the Kaiser company.

joint development program between Ford and the Thompson Products Co – with chief engineer Earl MacPherson obviously involved in the project. And it was MacPherson's name that was adopted to describe the new suspension – basically a refinement of earlier methods, not a completely different design – and the MacPherson Strut has become an automotive synonym, much like the domestic Hoover or Thermos names.

Superior engineering is all very well, but what the potential customer first sees when he enters the show room is the body of the automobile, not its chassis or suspension. But here too, the Lincoln was very highly thought of. The 1952 line represented the first cars that Lincoln-Mercury's chief stylist, William F. Schmidt, had directed from start to finish, and although George Walker was still retained by Ford as a styling consultant, he only seems to have had a limited input into the design work. The other in-house designers working with Schmidt were Don DeLaRossa (exteriors), L. David Ash (instru-

ment panels and details) and Don Beyreis (interiors and trim).

Following the Ford corporate styling theme, the Lincoln featured a more angular top half, emphasized on sedans and hardtops by a slightly flatter roof line and a greater area of glass. The prominent high set head lamps protruded over the bumper (in direct contrast to the recessed head lamps of the preceding models), adding to the aggressive look. The bumper itself was also positioned higher and did dual duty as the central bar of the grille opening. This integrated bumper-grille gave a very clean front end and was used by many other manufacturers in subsequent years.

A comprehensive brochure issued by Lincoln, detailing their success in the 1953 Carrera PanAmericana, carried the phrase "A Motor Car Revolution" on the cover. This was an exaggeration, and a tongue-in-cheek reference to the Mexican setting of the race, but in many ways the 1952-54 Lincolns were certainly evolutionary – so maybe we can forgive the word-play.

Below: Starfire was the new name for the Oldsmobile 98 convertible in '54 and it originally came from the Lockheed F-94 jet fighter, but was used on an Oldsmobile dream car displayed in '53. Apart from the obligatory annual body changes, the most noticeable styling feature is the Panoramic double curvature wrap-around windshield that appeared on all '54 Olds models. The Starfire engine was a 185 horsepower version of the 324 cu.in. Rocket V8 and 6,800 were sold, with a factory price of $3,248.

1955

Back in '55, cars were generally regarded as being for family use and categorized by body style – sedan, coupe, convertible or station wagon. If you wanted a sports car, you could look to Chevrolet's Corvette or to the Ford Thunderbird, or maybe even consider one of those itty-bitty European jobs. Combining the two as a sports-type passenger car wasn't really an option.

However, then came the Chrysler C-300. Styled by Virgil Exner, engineered by Robert M. Roger and powered by the legendary Chrysler FirePower Hemi V8, it was a revelation. Fast enough in standard form to set speed records over 127mph, and win NASCAR races when modified, the 2-door hardtop coupe could also seat six people in comfort. Part of the completely new-look Chrysler line in 1955, dubbed the "100 Million Dollar Look", it heralded a massive upturn in the marque's success as sales leapt an astounding 50% over the previous year.

At the very heart of the C-300 was the Hemi engine – so called because of its hemi-spherically-shaped combustion chambers – a configuration long regarded by engine experts as being the most efficient for producing maximum power. The problem with this design was that the valves were canted over at an angle to fit in to the hemi chamber and it required two rocker shafts and a complex arrangement of pushrods and varying lengths of rocker arms to make it work. This increased the cost of manufacturing the cylinder heads and the Hemi was replaced in 1959 by a more conventional wedge-head design.

Introduced in 1951, the Hemi displaced 331 cu.in. and pumped out an impressive 300 horsepower at 5,200rpm – providing the inspiration for the 300 Series name. As fitted to the '55 C-300, breathing through twin four-barrel carburetors with a full-race camshaft and an 8.5:1 compression ratio, the Hemi quickly earned Chrysler the "US Speed Champ" title. Naturally, the cars were great for racing and Tim Flock qualified a Chrysler on the pole at Daytona in 1955 and went on to win the race. He repeated the feat a year later and there's no doubt that the 300 Series would have been a major force in motor racing for some years if the manufacturers hadn't withdrawn it from competition in 1957.

The body design of the 1955 Chryslers evolved from a long line of concept cars built by Ghia in Italy under instruction from famed stylist Virgil Exner. The result was a complete break from Chrysler's previous "engineering-led" policy pursued by company president K. T. Keller, who had by now retired. His successor, Lester L. "Tex" Colbert, got rid of the old six cylinder engines and gave the styling department a freedom that was to produce some of the most striking automobiles of the Fifties under the "Forward Look" banner.

The C-300 was produced to compete with the limited-production Chevrolet Corvette and the Ford Thunderbird sports cars; not so

Below: Part of stylist Virgil Exner's new "One Hundred Million Dollar Look" for Chrysler, the C-300 was the high performance model of the 1955 range. It proved to be a race-winner and record setter, and was the first of the famed Letter Series of Chryslers, even though it didn't carry an "A" suffix. Only 1,725 of these 2-door hardtop coupes were built in '55.

Above: Elegance plus power brought a huge leap in sales of the main stream cars for Chrysler in '55, up by over 50%, but its image was undoubtedly helped by the achievements of the C-300 model. Embryonic tail fins were cleverly created by use of distinctive rear light housing and lens.

Above: The 300 model name came from the 300 brake horsepower produced by the 331 cu.in. FirePower V8 Hemi engine – so-called because of its hemispherical combustion chambers.

THE AMERICAN AUTOMOBILE

much for sales purposes, but more to improve Chrysler's performance image. Unable to create a special 2-seater model (although Ghia show cars of this configuration had been designed by Exner), Chrysler used what they had got. The starting point was a New Yorker 2-door hardtop body, with rear quarters from the Windsor and the grille from the Imperial to add prestige, although the New Yorker front bumper was retained.

The C-300 was a complete contrast to most other offerings of the time, when garish two-tone paint jobs and an excess of chrome was deemed the way to go. It had very little ornamentation, not even outside mirrors, and was only available in three colors – red, white and black. Even without its outstanding performance, this elegance would have set the C-300 apart from the rest. In 1955, this model represented status, luxury and performance in an exclusive package that was priced beyond the reach of the general public.

Rather surprisingly for such an expensive automobile (it was just about double the price of a Chevrolet or Ford), the C-300 didn't have air conditioning – even as a factory option. Another omission from the performance point of view was that the disc brakes used on the Imperial weren't included in the specification, although the drums all round with power assistance were thought to be more than adequate. Uprated springs and heavy duty shock absorbers helped put the cornering capability in a superior class when compared to the Chryler models, and a beefed-up PowerFlite automatic transmission with a higher stall speed torque converter produced rapid acceleration – 0-60mph in under 10 seconds.

Options such as power steering, power windows, radio, heater, tinted glass, and four-way power adjustable front bench seat could all be used to enhance the tan leather and vinyl trimmed interior. Regarded as highly desirable today, was the possibility of having

Right: Chevrolet had a banner year in '55, thanks to a totally redesigned car and a brilliant new V8 engine. This Bel Air convertible was chosen as the Pace Car for the Indy 500, and put Chevrolet at the top of the sales charts with over 1.7 million sales – a record for any auto manufacturer at the time.

Below: The Packard Caribbean convertible had attractive new body lines, but they covered an old floor pan. With powerful 275bhp, 352 cu.in. V8 and Twin Ultramatic transmission plus a unique torsion bar suspension, the '55 Packard was something special. But production difficulties were to prove a major setback and only 500 were built.

Kelsey-Hayes wire wheels fitted at a whopping $600 a set.

It goes without saying that this exclusivity would result in very few C-300 models being produced, only 1,725 in fact, and it is estimated that there are approximately two hundred survivors. But the influence of the C-300 went far beyond mere sales figures. It was to be the founding member of a legendary automotive dynasty – the so-called Letter Series Chryslers. Following the favorable reactions from the media to the '55 offering, the following year a face-lifted 1956 version was designated the 300B. This became an annual feature of the Chrysler model line-up, with a change of suffix letter, until the final 300L in 1965 – although the 300 Series itself lasted as a distinct model group until 1971.

As was the trend, all American automobiles were getting longer, lower and wide and size was an important aspect of the C-300 (and all the other 1955 Chrysler models). However, the extra inches on length and width had some unforeseen side effects. While a three inch longer car might not make much difference parked on the driveway, nose-to-tail on the assembly line it soon added up and manufacturers found themselves having to extend their production lines by up to 30 feet to accommodate the new designs. Police and city officials also voiced doubts over how these bigger cars were going to fit into existing parking places.

In purely economic terms, 1955 was a boom year in the auto industry with nearly 8 million cars being churned out by Detroit. Disneyland opened in California, the rock 'n' roll era arrived with Bill Haley and his Comets topping the charts with "Rock Around The Clock" and the minimum wage was raised to $1 per hour. On the flip side, Martin Luther King was leading a bus boycott in Alabama protesting against segregation, and James Dean died in an auto accident.

There were many great cars made that year, but the merits of the Chrysler FirePower Hemi engine cannot be denied and, equally, it is impossible to ignore the sheer class of Virgil Exner's design. If ever there was a prize for the perfect combination of performance and appearance, then the '55 Chrysler C-300 must surely rank as one of the top contenders of all time.

Below: The 1955 Cadillac sales brochure simply oozes class and style, as befits such a luxury automobile and status symbol. The tempting cover strap line of "Just imagine it's yours!" is matched by the equally evocative phrases inside, including: "Perhaps it's time to stop dreaming about a Cadillac and start enjoying one!" – back in 1955, plenty of people did just that, and who can blame them?

Just imagine it's yours!

1956

We like Ike. That was the message resounding through the nation as Dwight Eisenhower was returned for a second term as President in a landslide victory over Adlai Stevenson. Yet to be crowned "The King", Elvis Presley was hitting the charts and grabbing headlines thanks to songs like "Heartbreak Hotel", "Don't Be Cruel" and "Blue Suede Shoes". Another title holder, world heavyweight boxing champion Rocky Marciano, announced his retirement from the ring.

The phrase "cause and effect" is something that comes to mind when looking at Ford's Thunderbird. That it was made in response to arch rival Chevrolet bringing out the Corvette isn't in doubt, but that it would also have the consequence of ensuring the survival of the GM model was certainly something that was far from Ford's intention. It is also ironic that, having rescued the Corvette from oblivion and provided evidence of a viable market for a US-built sports car, the Thunderbird would quickly be taken out of that sector and turned into a luxury four-seater.

The reason for the decision was numbers, and it proved to be a correct direction for the second generation Thunderbird to take in 1958, but that's taking us away from the original concept. There is a story that the idea for the T-Bird first came about following the visit by Ford general manager Lewis D. Crusoe and styling consultant George Walker to the 1951 Paris Auto Show in France. Seeing all the European sports cars on display, Crusoe is supposed to have asked Walker why Ford didn't have anything similar, and the consultant (probably to keep his paymaster happy) replied that they were already working on just such a design. Immediately following this conversation, Walker was then said to have phoned his office back in the USA and told them to get something put together in time for his return.

It seems unlikely that these events ever actually happened. George Walker was a deft manipulator of the facts and often claimed credit for car design work that he personally was only involved with on an administration level. It has also to be remembered that there were an awful lot of young designers in the industry and their enthusiasm for the sports car would have generated many illustrations and drawings on the "what if we built one of those?" basis. Therefore, it can be assumed

that Ford (in common with most other manufacturers) had, over the years, been carrying out various design studies on sports cars but not progressed them any further because of the perceived limited sales potential.

When Chevrolet brought out the Corvette in 1953, Ford had to respond quickly, and unveiled a full-size wood and clay mock-up of the Thunderbird at the Detroit Auto Show in February 1954. At a press conference held in the Ford Styling Rotunda at Dearborn, Ford's sales manager L. W. Smead announced: "The Thunderbird is a new kind of sports car. We are convinced it will set a new trend in the automobile industry. It provides all of the comforts, conveniences and all-weather protection available in any of today's modern

1956

Below: Several changes were made to 1956 Thunderbirds following feedback from owners of '55 models. The externally-mounted spare wheel is the most obvious feature – intended to give more luggage space in the trunk – but weight distribution was affected. Other alterations to improve driver comfort included wind wings on the windshield to prevent buffeting when enjoying topless motoring, and vent doors in the front fenders to feed fresh air into the passenger compartment. The rear bumper also had exhausts exiting through slots in the corners.

Above: Following the merger with Nash in 1954 to form American Motors Corporation, Hudson models became little more than Nash bodies with different grilles, interiors and rear ends. This 1956 Hudson Hornet Custom Hollywood hardtop coupe illustrates just how disastrous the marriage turned out to be as, in an attempt to provide a separate identity, so called "V-line" styling was used with bizarre results. Not surprisingly, sales dropped and only 10,671 Hudson models (excluding rebadged Ramblers) were produced in '56 and the Hudson name was dropped the following year.

automobiles. It represents a successful combination of graceful, low-silhouette styling, spirited performance and outstanding roadability with dependable all-steel body construction."

The references to the Corvette's features are obvious enough. In addition, the T-Bird came with a V8 engine and the choice of manual or automatic transmission, an attractive glass fiber removable hardtop, wind-up windows (power optional) and, using standard Ford components, it could be serviced at a regular dealership.

Production of the Thunderbird wasn't due to begin until September 1954, by which time Ford were placing much more emphasis on the level of driver and passenger comfort than speed or handling when discussing the model, possibly giving a slight hint of where the company thought its future might lay. W. R. Burnett, chief of passenger car engineering said: "Although the Thunderbird has the performance and attributes of most sports cars, management also felt that it should have a few more comforts to make it more appealing

to a wider segment of the public." Burnett also used the term "personal car" to describe the T-Bird, this being Ford's way of elevating it above the other run-of-the-mill sports cars.

Compared to the Corvette, Thunderbird sales were incredible – almost 16,000 a year in 1955 and '56, compared to a paltry 700 1955 Corvettes and only 3,400 of the revamped '56. It was clear that Ford had a better grasp of what the American buyer of the Fifties wanted from a sports car.

In this respect, a great deal of the credit for the Thunderbird's acceptance must go to Ford's chief of styling Frank Q. Hershey and his design studio team, headed by Rhys Miller. Also involved in the creation of the T-Bird were Damon Woods, David Ash and Bill Boyer. Between them, they produced a car that echoed the best features of European sports car design yet could be easily identified as American in origin with immediate connection to the rest of the Ford model line-up. Key elements were the proportions of a long hood and short rear deck, combined

Above: From the start, the Lincoln Continental Mark II was hailed as a truly classic automobile. It was an attempt by Ford to create an image car that would outshine the best Cadillacs. Unfortunately, Ford lost money on every Mark II it produced.

Below: Buicks had a mild face-lift for '56, and came with more powerful engines. About 635,000 rolled off the assembly lines in 1956; how many of them ended up like this we wonder?

with the low profile found in all classic Fifties front-engined sports cars, plus embellishments that could only have come from Detroit.

But Hershey and his designers weren't infallible and for the '56 Thunderbird, there were a few minor alterations that had to be carried out for purely practical reasons. The most easily-spotted of the changes was the Continental Kit mounting of the spare wheel to make more trunk space available for luggage, but this wasn't universally approved of, indeed some critics said it detracted from the car's appearance and added wind resistance.

On the other hand, this set-up was also said to help give a better balanced weight distribution. Small vent door flaps were introduced behind the front wheel arches to feed the interior with cool air after complaints from overheating drivers and passengers! In a similar vein, "wind wings" were added to the sides of the windshield to help reduce buffeting when the top was down.

If you chose to drive with the hardtop in position, in '56 this would more than likely come with the famous portholes on either side. These little round windows were apparently copied from car designs of the 1930s, and some writers have said that Bill Boyer was the man behind this idea. Non-porthole hardtops were still available but the porthole version offered as a no cost option proved to be far more popular and has become indelibly associated with the '56 T-Bird.

Long forgotten, is the fact that Ford were also using safety as a selling point in those days. Okay, maybe a Life Guard package consisting of a collapsible steering column and anti-burst door locks isn't in the same league as dual air bags, but we are talking 1956 here! The offer of seat belts was another item that didn't prove too enticing to potential buyers, who were more likely to ask, "Why are you fitting seat belts – isn't the car safe?" How times have changed!

American Indian folklore was said to describe the Thunderbird as a good luck omen, being a mythical bird supposed to cause thunder, lightning and rain. A 1954 Ford press release went on to state that, among many things, the Thunderbird symbolised 'power, swiftness and prosperity'. If that is true, then Ford could hardly have picked a more appropriate name.

1957

Headlines were dominated by racial integration conflicts, the radio was reverberating to the sound of rock 'n' roll and Russia launched Sputnik 1 to take a commanding lead in the space race. Hollywood mourned the deaths of silver screen idol Humphrey Bogart and comedian Oliver Hardy. But in the realm of automotive history, 1957 will forever be the year of the Chevrolet Bel Air.

In terms of styling, the 1957 Chevrolet is almost a unique example, for it has enjoyed undiminished affection since its introduction. It has been the subject of numerous songs, featured in films whenever a Fifties classic is required and was once dubbed "the most popular used car in history". Today, four decades on, there are enough suppliers of restoration and reproduction parts that it is practically possible to build a complete new car. Surely no other car from the 1950s can boast such an enthusiastic following.

A look at the outline specification doesn't explain the reasons behind this phenomenon – a face-lift of a three year old bodyshell and a smaller V8 engine than both the Ford and Plymouth rivals – but that simplistic descrip-

Below: The swept-back tail fins and ribbed silver anodised aluminum fender trim accentuate the sweeping lines of the '57 Chevy Bel Air. The gold V on the trunk lid indicates that the car has a V8 engine, the potent Turbo-Fire 283 cu.in. unit. As with the front, the rear bumper is a more integrated part of the body design and incorporates the tail lights in bold clusters. The fender skirts were optional extras.

tion doesn't do the '57 Chevy justice. It is, quite simply, a styling and performance classic. Not that this was apparent to the designers and engineers working on the car, far from it. In fact, studio head Clare MacKichan has been quoted as saying that there didn't seem to be much continuity of thought from one year to the next, and even some of the ideas that weren't used on the 1956 models somehow got resurrected and put on the '57!

The massive new front bumper had even earlier origins, with sketches dating back to 1949 and in 1953, designer Carl Renner produced an illustration that looked almost identical to the final '57 bumper. Apart from the bumper and front end, perhaps the most striking aspect of the 1957 Chevrolet is just how much longer and lower it seems in comparison to the previous two years, despite sharing the same basic bodyshell. This was due

to Earl's quest to reduce height and increase length in the belief that it produced a better looking automobile. To keep the cowl profile low, a revolutionary ventilation system was devised which drew fresh air from inlets in the front fenders above the headlights, rather than at the base of the windshield.

The hood had dual lance-shaped "windsplitz" instead of the typical central jet aircraft-style ornament, used by other cars, for a low, smooth look. Elsewhere, the body revamp for '57 was so clever that, not only did it look different to the 1956 models, it was considered a great improvement. Undoubtedly one of the Fifties' most memorable and recognizable styling details is the ribbed aluminum panel used as part of the rear fender decorative trim on the Bel Air – it is an image, almost a trademark or a logo that couldn't be mistaken for anything else.

Above: Among the most striking features on the 1957 Bel Air was the massive front bumper, which became an integral part of the body shape rather than an add-on. The convertible shows the low profile to great effect; the hood height was reduced by introducing fresh air vents above the headlights and eliminating the need for intake at the base of the windshield. In place of the traditional central hood emblem, twin spears also helped achieve the lower look.

The other big news for the '57 Chevy was the engine and fuel injection. With a .125 inch diameter bigger bore, the small block V8 now displaced 283 cu.in. and was becoming a high performance legend. In standard two-barrel carburettor form, the compact power-plant was rated at a healthy 185 horsepower and, when equipped with fuel injection, the Chevy could produce one horsepower per cubic inch which was an accomplishment at the time, although Chrysler had done the same with the FirePower Hemi engine somewhat earlier. It meant a very rapid car in a straight line – even a base V8 model with a Powerglide two-speed automatic could top 100mph and accelerate to 60mph in 11 seconds.

Priced at over $500 (very expensive in '57 when a basic Chevrolet was little more than $2,000) the optional Ramjet mechanical fuel injection unit initially looked like a technical innovation, claimed to improve fuel economy as well as horsepower. Designed by GM and made by Rochester Carburetor Inc, after they had tested and modified it, in everyday use the Ramjet started to show problems. In particular, the fuel nozzles would get clogged and heat absorption from the engine caused rough idling. So the fuel injection option was dropped from the Chevrolet family car catalog after 1958, although an improved version remained as a Corvette item until 1965.

Another unsuccessful Chevy development in '57 was the Turboglide automatic transmission. Modeled on the Buick Dynaflow, it was more expensive to make than the existing Powerglide unit and, while smoother-shifting when performing properly, it proved less reliable and hard to repair when faults occurred. The Turboglide lasted better than the Ramjet, surviving until the end of the '61 model year, but both ventures were only relatively minor blemishes on the

record of an automotive masterpiece.

It seems strange then to learn that, in 1957, Chevrolet failed to dominate the new car market in the same way as before. In fact, taking model year sales into account, Ford took first place. Competition was fiercer than ever and despite price reductions, '57 was not the great year the auto industry had anticipated. Indeed, come the fourth quarter of the year, the beginnings of the economic slump that was to devastate US car sales in 1958 started to have an effect and demand fell sharply.

Another blow to Chevrolet came when the Automobile Manufacturers Association passed a resolution in June forbidding their members

Above: Similarities between the Oldsmobile Holiday sedan and the Chevy are obvious, but the Olds looks more refined. One curious feature is the three-piece backlight which seems in contrast to the huge double curvature windshield and hardtop style.

Below: A spectacular debutante in '57 was the Ford Fairlane 500 Skyliner retractable hardtop. At the touch of a button, the steel roof would fold into the trunk turning coupe into convertible. Its complexity and high cost limited production to just three years.

"Appreciably faster on all counts" and, in a test carried out by the same magazine later in the year, the Chevy came out ahead of both Ford and Plymouth. Fast cars gave rise to doubts about people's ability to cope, however. James Whipple of Car Life suggested that drivers would need "quicker reactions and better judgement than ever before", but concluded: "Beneath the excitement created by the sensational (for light, low-priced cars) horsepower, the '57 Chevy is an excellent automobile with a tested, stable design and a very satisfactory level of quality and workmanship".

With all this talk of power, it is easy to forget that Chevrolet then offered three models – starting with the One-Fifty, Two-Ten, and top of the range Bel Air – and the cheaper models came with much less horsepower. And while today's collector car money would go on the more expensive Bel Air coupes and convertibles, in 1957 it was the 4-door sedans that sold better than anything else.

Above: Another first for Ford in '57 was the Ranchero, a sedan-pickup which basically came from a standard Ranch Wagon station wagon with the rear half converted into an open bed. This set a trend for further car-based trucks in the American market that were to prove popular for many years to come.

to participate in motor racing. However, while the men in the Chevy front office were following the AMA ruling and stating "they were no longer in racing", there was plenty of help out of the back door for those drivers who could put a Chevrolet into the winner's circle.

Using a racing driver to test a model was a device used by magazines in the Fifties, and Speed Age got stock car ace Johnnie Tolan to test a '57 Bel Air 4-door sedan on the track and in the Los Angeles traffic. He reported: "I was really impressed with the new Chevy – liked its looks as well as its performance…" Journalist Walt Woron writing for Motor Trend also liked the Chevy's performance, calling it

Right: Plymouths were totally redone for '57, and many people regard them to be among the best designs ever produced by Virgil Exner. The low, clean lines, huge expanses of glass and the tallest tail fins on offer put them ahead of the competition in many respects. The Fury 2-door hardtop coupe had unique gold anodised aluminum Sport Tone body trim panels, upswept front bumper ends, a 290 horsepower V8 and other extra embellishments to denote its top-of-the-range status.

1958

The banner headline in the Detroit Free Press read "Reds claim their missile can reach the whole world" as America was smarting after the Sputniks demonstrated the Soviet lead in the space race, but the main picture on the newspaper's front page was of an Edsel. However, the economy was in recession and car sales in '58 dropped by about 20% compared with the three previous boom years.

In automotive terms, the Edsel name has become associated with spectacular failure – almost since it was launched in September 1957. Yet the surprise is, the Edsel disaster happened not by chance, but following years of solid market research and meticulous planning by the Ford Motor Company.

At the start of the 1950s, it seemed to Ford that it didn't offer enough models to cover the entire market and was losing out in certain sectors, particularly the middle price bracket. Back then, if an owner was happy with a car they would buy a replacement from the same manufacturer. And if they had become more prosperous (or just wanted to give the neighbors the impression that they had – keeping up with the Joneses was quite an obsession that the dealers happily exploited), they traded up to a more expensive, and therefore more prestigious, make from the same corporation.

According to a company executive: "Ford

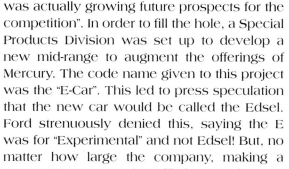

was actually growing future prospects for the competition". In order to fill the hole, a Special Products Division was set up to develop a new mid-range to augment the offerings of Mercury. The code name given to this project was the "E-Car". This led to press speculation that the new car would be called the Edsel. Ford strenuously denied this, saying the E was for "Experimental" and not Edsel! But, no matter how large the company, making a 100% new car is unlikely to make economic sense so the E-Car was planned as a hybrid of existing Ford and Mercury major components with its own front and rear end sheet metal, its own engine, interior and dash panels.

The one thing the E-Car wouldn't share would be the Ford or Lincoln-Mercury dealerships, it would have its very own sales network. A vast recruiting campaign was organised and dealers were signed up from competitors across the country.

The pressure was now on to give the car a name. Over six thousand suggestions were considered from all sorts of sources – including poet Marianne Moore who came up with humdingers like "Mongoose Civique" and "Utopian Turtletop"! Four names that got a more favorable reaction were: Ranger, Pacer, Corsair and Citation. Although these were eventually chosen as the model names, Ford chairman Ernest Breech didn't like them or any of the alternatives and, early in 1956, he made the decision to call the car the Edsel – named after Henry Ford's son who had died in 1942. Initially the Ford family were against the suggestion, but Breech persuaded them.

This choice of name was the first mistake. Outside Detroit's inner circle, the word Edsel had no significance. While certainly no worse than Buick, that General Motors marque had, by then, been in existence for over fifty years and was well established in people's minds.

Then came the second mistake. The Edsel had probably the biggest new car build-up in history. The publicity was so widespread that the public were expecting a miracle machine to appear, not just another new car.

The third problem with the Edsel was timing, and this would prove to be crucial. The plan was to launch the 1958 Edsels in June 1957, thereby pre-empting the competition – traditionally cars were launched between September and November. But Edsel production didn't start until July and the launch was put back until September to ensure that dealers would have cars on display for the big day.

This three month delay was a huge setback. After strong early 1957 model sales, the market suddenly slowed up in midsummer and dealers had to offer discounts to clear stocks and make way for the new '58 models. The US economy went into recession and the demand for middle- to upper-priced cars evaporated in favor of smaller, cheaper

Above: Probably the most hyped car in history, the Edsel was a gigantic disaster for Ford. The unusual "horse collar" grille was blamed for the lack of sales, but the car was introduced just when market for larger, more expensive cars went into decline.

Left: The convertible Edsel looks sleek in side view, and certainly no worse than any contemporary models. The Pacer version was in the next range up from the basic Ranger specification, having more chrome trim, extra equipment and slightly plusher upholstery.

Right: An extensive advertising campaign was mounted and in '59, one slogan used was: "The car that makes history by making sense" – the Edsel certainly made history, but for all the wrong reasons.

Right: The proud history of Packard ended in 1958. Among the last was the Hawk 2-door hardtop coupe – a Studebaker body with a glass fiber front (Packard had bought Studebaker in 1954), and a rather bizarre optional extra of padded armrests on the outside of the doors! Only 588 were built.

Below: The Cadillac Eldorado Biarritz convertible featured special rounded off rear deck and fender panels plus big shark fins. Plenty of superfluous brightwork included dummy louvers in front of the rear wheels and fake air intake on the front fender; quad head lights were standard on all '58s.

models. So, at the very time the Edsel burst on the scene, the market went into a severe decline. In other words, the goal posts had been moved! Despite these three problems, the Edsel could still have succeeded. And Ford's need for the car was still valid. But the final blow was the controversial styling.

The most famous feature is the "horse collar"

grille. Although many European marques had a vertical grille for many years – Jaguar, Alfa Romeo, Mercedes – somehow the Edsel didn't have the same effect.

When an automobile is successful, people clamor to associate themselves with it. In the case of the Edsel, practically everyone who worked at the Ford Design Center denies any

Above: A rare Rambler Ambassador 4-door hardtop station wagon. The decision to drop the Nash and Hudson names was last minute and the factory often airbrushed badges out of the publicity photos. The Rambler wagon did not sell and only 294 were built – perhaps due to the weird pillarless style and mishmash of design features.

involvement with it. The man responsible was Roy A. Brown, promoted to chief designer of the E-Car project following his successful work on the Lincoln Futura show car. He recruited Bob Jones, Dick Steiger and Bert Holmes as his assistants. The team decided to go away from the horizontal grille with a wide opening used by most of the other marques and opted for the vertical look.

Enthusiastic approval for the concept was given by a gathering of top Ford executives in August 1955 and, from then on, the die was cast. On launch day, it seemed the Edsel was a winner as 2.5 million people crowded to see the new car. After a few days, the first alarm bells rang – everybody came to look, but nobody was buying. After predictions of over a quarter of a million sales in the first

year, only 63,110 were ever produced.

The Edsel was discontinued in November 1959, after two years, two months and fifteen days. It was estimated to have cost Ford over 350 million dollars. Henry Ford II typically took it on the chin and said afterwards: "Hell, we headed right into a recession, and everything went kaput... A lot of people didn't like the styling of the Edsel. We had a very weak dealer organisation...we couldn't sell them, we were losing money, so we made a decision, 'Let's quit' which was the right decision, I'm sure. I'd rather admit the mistake, chop it off, and don't throw good money after bad."

Since the demise of the Edsel, people have suggested bizarre reasons for its failure. A few years ago, one psychologist even went so far as to claim that the real reason for the Edsel catastrophe was that the horse collar grille represented the female sex organ, while all the other automobiles were masculine!

The real reason for the failure of the Edsel is simple. The combination of recession, too much hype, a poor choice of name and peculiar styling proved insurmountable. However, had Ford seen it through those initial dark days and kept it going until the market swung back in favor of bigger, more expensive cars in the Sixties – who knows? We might still have been able to buy an Edsel today.

What was the Edsel really like as a car? In truth it was no better, no worse than its contemporaries. And that probably says it all.

Right: The Corvette had four head lights in '58, the body was 3 inches wider, 10 inches longer and weighed 100 pounds more, but sales leapt by 50% despite the recession. The front grille had nine teeth instead of thirteen, but best news was a fuel-injected 290 horsepower version of the 283 cu.in. V8 which did 0-60mph in 6.9 seconds.

1959

The history of the twentieth century is, more often than not, divided up into decades and each ten year period given its own separate identity. It is curious that this convenient method of grouping so often, and in so many ways, reflects the changes that take place in society. In purely automotive terms, nothing can surely equal the 1959 Cadillac tail fin as a symbol of the end of an era.

The Fifties was the age of the tail fin and, after having reached such heights, there was nowhere to go but down. 1959 was also the year that Harley Earl retired from his position as head of styling at General Motors and the towering Cadillac fins are looked upon as his final extravagance before bowing out. It has to be said that Earl would have found it hard to adapt to a changing environment of simplicity and economy rather than outrageous, ever bigger automobiles. It was a problem that other designers, working at rival auto makers, would also struggle to come to terms with.

At the time, there were few, if any, signs of misgivings. Designer Bill Mitchell (who took over from Earl) described the tail fins thus: "From a design standpoint the fins gave definition to the rear of the car for the first time. They made the back end as interesting as the front, and established a long-standing Cadillac styling hallmark." Whether the addition of a rear "grille" which closely resembled that of the front was such a good idea is open to debate, but the feature didn't last very long.

Lower than ever before, though no longer or wider, the '59 Cadillac not only attracted comments about its styling it also drew some favorable reports about how it drove. Jim Whipple, writing in Car Life, said: "The car rode as level as any I've ever driven..." But it wasn't totally perfect, as shown by a report in Motor Life which stated: "Flaws are noted only at high speeds, when some swaying motion sets in, and in fast corners when the tires protest loudly as the heavyweight goes through a bend". Of course, the Cadillac was built for luxury motoring and comfort, and not intended for slalom racing, so it can be safely assumed that few were ever pushed to the same limits by their owners.

Mind you, thanks to a new 325 horsepower (345hp in Eldorado models), 390 cu.in. V8 engine under that hood, the Cadillac was no slouch when it was time to get going, 0-60mph in under 11 seconds or thereabouts. And if you were in a real hurry, a top speed of close on 120mph was possible. Pretty impressive for a car weighing over 5,000 pounds and close to 19 feet in length. Sales moved ahead too, topping 142,000 and keeping Cadillac in the top ten (just) of US auto manufacturers.

The array of Cadillac models included convertibles, two-door hardtop coupes, and two different four-door hardtop sedans plus the Fleetwood limousines. Prices started at about $5000 and went up to $7400 for an Eldorado,

Below: The convertible '59 Cadillac looked like a de luxe rocket ship. The grille featured double-decker construction with mirror-image quad head lights incorporated into a massive bumper. The series 62 was the lowest priced, but standard equipment included power steering, power brakes, automatic transmission, windshield washers and two-speed wipers. 11,130 were produced.

Right: The rear of the '59 Cadillac is unique thanks to soaring razor-edged fins with four bullet-shaped tail lights, and there has surely never been a more distinctive styling feature on any automobile in history. But the Harley Earl trademark had reached its limit and would shortly disappear with the coming of a new decade and a growing demand for less ostentatious and more economical cars.

with the Fleetwoods more than $9,500. But easily the most expensive was the Eldorado Brougham 4-door, the only Cadillac model of '59 that didn't have the huge tail fins and bullet-shaped lights, which was built by coach builders Pininfarina in Italy, and cost a massive $13,000 – small wonder that only 99 made the transatlantic crossing this year. But underneath all the razzle-dazzle there were engineering improvements too, with better suspension, and revised power steering.

In May 1959, Motor Life compared the Cadillac to an Imperial and summed up with the following: "Cadillac's strongest claim to superiority is its unmatched feeling of luxury and quality. When riding in this car, the almost soundless operation coupled with rich materials and fine assembly produce the desired effect: you know that this is an expensive and luxurious automobile. One is never in doubt".

A smooth ride, luxury fitments, excellent performance and build quality – from almost any aspect, the 1959 Cadillac was a state-of-the-art prestige car of its day, but you cannot ignore the flamboyant body styling. Whatever your personal tastes, this is one car that it is impossible to be neutral about, you either love it or loathe it.

To its detractors, the '59 Caddy has all the glamor of a Las Vegas hooker, while others regard it as the ultimate expression of Fifties space age design. Its styling is unique and the obvious associations with rockets, missiles and aircraft are clearly visible – from the dual jet intake shapes of the parking lights in the massive front bumper to the bullet-like tail

lights (said to represent exhaust flames) set in those soaring fins. It is a triumph of design over function. Nobody needed fins that tall, nor the lavish application of chrome, nor most of the other styling excesses included under Harley Earl's direction.

However, need and want are two entirely different emotions and Earl was a master at producing automobiles that were wanted in the highly prosperous USA of the Fifties. True, his obsessive pursuit of getting a car as low as possible had created designs that were at, or very near, the minimum height possible – given the agility of the average human being and ease of entry and exit required. And who knows how many knees were bruised in consequence, particularly negotiating a way around the bottom corner of the wrap-around windshields (another Harley Earl innovation) that protruded into the access opening. Ergonomics came second to styling, and

Above top: Awarded the Gold Medal for Exceptional Styling at the World Fair in Brussels, '59 Fords have often been touted as the most beautiful cars of the Fifties. This is the Fairlane 500 Club Victoria 2-door hardtop.

Above: The low-slung Pontiac Bonneville was quite a performance machine and helped promote a more youthful image for the marque, which moved from sixth to third place in the sales charts over the next three years.

Far left: Chevrolet finally caught up with Ford's Ranchero when it launched the El Camino in '59. Designed along the same Vista-top lines as the regular Chevys, the El Camino was based on the base model Biscayne Brook wood station wagon.

131

THE AMERICAN AUTOMOBILE

Above: The Fifties yellow Checker taxi is part of New York's image. There are now few working and many, like this one, have been relegated to static promotional tasks.

Right: The smoothly-styled '59 Buick Electra 225 convertible had fifty chrome rectangles in its grille, but this was about the only styling connection with preceding years' models.

product liability litigation was nothing like the rapacious industry of the Nineties so such small inconveniences as these would be tolerated for the sake of owning the newest shape of automobile.

The annual model change that ultimately spawned the '59 Cadillac was regarded as part of the process that would provide what the Detroit public relations machine called "better transportation tomorrows". A false promise if ever there was one because, as every child knows, tomorrow never arrives. We can look at these things with the condescension of hindsight, but caught up in the euphoria of the age it was hard to be completely objective. Without doubt, Car Life's Jim Whipple echoed popular opinion when he enthusiastically described the '59 Cadillac as "...one of the sleekest jobs that ever came down the pike".

But to many fans, 1959 marked the beginning of the end of rock 'n' roll, and the most significant event of the year happened on February 3rd when a Beechcraft Bonanza light aeroplane crashed near Mason City, Iowa killing Buddy Holly, Ritchie Valens and J. P. "The Big Bopper" Richardson. However, if three stars had been extinguished from the pop music firmament, at least there were two new stars on Old Glory as Alaska and Hawaii became the 49th and 50th States. And NASA was also aiming towards the stars, besides launching satellites and two monkeys into orbit, it also named the seven astronauts who would take part in the space race.

Automobiles might be about to get their wings clipped and the raw energy of Fifties rock 'n' rollers seemed to be giving way to slushy music exploited by large record companies in pursuit of a quick buck, but there was still plenty to look forward to!

1960

The Fifties had been a great time for the American auto industry – a period of design excess, during which automobiles grew ever larger fins and literally dripped with chrome. But as the new decade of the Sixties dawned, things were changing, the emphasis would switch from overstated looks to more efficient performance, whether it be from smaller cars or bigger engines.

Changes in the auto industry were not the only news for 1960. In July, John F. Kennedy received the Democratic nomination for the Presidency, running against Republican Richard Nixon. Kennedy made it to The White House after a close race, but was tragically not to serve his full term. Meanwhile, relations with the Soviet Union received a major setback when a U2 spy plane was shot down over Soviet territory and its pilot, Gary Powers, captured. On a lighter note, Elvis Presley was discharged from his much-publicized spell in the US Army, while a young boxer by the name of Cassius Clay won a gold medal in the Rome Olympics. He would become one of the most famous boxers of all time, who would ultimately be known to millions around the world as Muhammed Ali.

Lovers of speed had plenty to talk about, too. At the Daytona 500, Fireball Roberts, driving a '60 Pontiac, had set the pace during qualifying at 151.556mph, while the race proper was won by Junior Johnson in a 1959 Chevy. Pontiac products also featured prominently at the Bonneville Salt Flats in September, when hot rodder Mickey Thompson drove his Challenger streamliner to a speed of 406.60mph. The sleek projectile was powered by no less than four Pontiac V8s, but a broken driveshaft prevented him from making a return run that would have put him in the record books.

Back in Detroit, however, high-performance automobiles were not the latest innovation from the major manufacturers – they would come later in the decade. For 1960, the auto industry was looking in a completely different direction. Since the 1930s, American automobiles had grown steadily larger, particularly in the post-war years. But during that time, small imported cars had begun to make inroads on the market, particularly sporty

Below: The air-cooled, rear-engine layout of Chevrolet's Corvair was unfamiliar to potential buyers. Only when it was marketed as a sporty compact did it begin to succeed.

models. They were fun to drive and cheap to run. Concerned by the impact these foreign cars were making, the major auto makers began to take a serious look at building more compact cars themselves. By the late Fifties, two smaller manufacturers were already in this sector of the market – Studebaker with the Lark, and Rambler with the American. In 1960, they would be joined by compacts from the big three – Ford, GM and Chrysler – who launched the Falcon, the Chevrolet Corvair and the Valiant respectively.

Of the three, the Falcon and the Corvair were the main contenders and were pitted against each other from the outset. They were two very different cars, the Ford simply being a scaled-down conventional car, while the Chevy was very definitely a radical departure in terms of both design and powerplant. Both had their beginnings in the mid Fifties and, more by accident than design, they both arrived on the market at the same time.

One aspect that was common to the Falcon and Corvair was unibody construction, a relatively uncommon arrangement for American automobiles at the time which, in the main, relied on separate chassis to sup-

port the various mechanical components and body panels. In a unibody design, the bodyshell itself is strengthened to accept the loads of the engine and suspension, making for a lighter structure overall. However, that is where the similarities ended.

As mentioned, the Falcon was of a conventional design. It was powered by a liquid-cooled, straight-six ohv engine, with a cast-iron block and head, that displaced 144.3 cu.in. and developed 90 horsepower at 4200rpm. This drove through either a three-speed manual transmission or two-speed automatic to a live rear axle suspended on leaf springs. The Corvair was also powered by a six-cylinder engine, but it was a horizontally-opposed, aluminum, air-cooled unit mounted at the rear of the car and driving the rear wheels through a three-speed manual, or two-speed automatic, transaxle with coil-sprung, swing-axle suspension. The engine produced 80 horsepower at 4400rpm. Both cars had similar front suspension arrangements, making use of unequal-length wishbones and coil springing.

The cars were of similar sizes, although the Falcon was slightly larger and taller, and

Above: Ford's European experience of building small cars led to the Falcon compact, with its unibody construction. Later sporty versions provided the basis for the Mustang.

both were intended as full six-seaters, being equipped with bench seats front and rear. However, the Falcon's transmission tunnel made it uncomfortable for anyone riding in the middle of the front seat, while the Corvair, with its virtually flat floorpan, was more comfortable, even though the manual transmission models had a floor-mounted shifter. This was curved to allow the center passenger leg room. Shifting was not a problem in the Falcon, since both manual and automatic transmissions had column shifters.

When first launched, the Corvair was offered in a 4-door body style only, while the Falcon came in a choice of 2- or 4-door models. The latter was conventional in appear-

Below: Compare the body style of this Pontiac Catalina convertible with that of the Oldsmobile Super 88 opposite. Fenders and trim panels may differ, but the shell is the same.

ance, while the Corvair, with its lack of radiator grille and somewhat tub-like styling, was less so. Both lacked the fins and chrome that had characterized cars of the Fifties. They were intended as economy cars and they looked the part.

In terms of performance, the makers quoted very similar top speeds – 87mph for the Falcon; 88mph for the Corvair. But the Falcon could out-accelerate the Corvair; Road & Track magazine found that the former could reach 60mph in 17.7 seconds, while the Corvair was nearly a full two seconds behind at 19.5 seconds.

When the Corvair was launched, it was slow to gain acceptance; the unconventional

Above: Oldsmobile's Super 88 Celebrity sedan looks similar to Chevy's Impala but, mechanically, it differed with a choice of two V8s and a three-speed manual transmission.

rear-engine layout may have been okay in a foreign car, but it was downright un-American; the Falcon was a much more familiar concept, and it showed in the sales figures. Corvair sales were not helped by rumors that it tended to throw fan belts and that its handling was quirky. Indeed, if the tire pressures were not kept exactly as specified by the manufacturer and the car was pushed hard through a corner, it could switch from slight understeer to strong oversteer, kicking the rear end out with potentially disastrous consequences. Later in its life, a number of law suits were brought against GM for just this reason, although eventually the car was exonerated and would carry on in production until the end of the decade.

Later in 1960, in an attempt to boost flagging sales, Chevrolet introduced a 2-door variant, the Monza. This was a much sportier-looking car, a look that was enhanced by fitting front bucket seats, full carpeting and better trim. Where the Corvair had failed as an economy car, it succeeded as a sporty model and sales took off at last. Eventually, it was to receive ever more powerful engines and became an excellent all-round performer. Not to be outdone, Ford uprated later models of the Falcon too, eventually fitting a new 260 cu.in. small-block V8 that was to have a significant effect on the company's efforts in the sporty compact field.

Left: Fins and chrome still featured on another Chrysler product, the Plymouth Fury. Although incorporating the modern unibody construction, the old "jukebox on wheels" style led to poor sales of their 1960 models.

1961

Recycling is a familiar theme of the 1990s, and many of today's manufacturers emphasize how much material in their cars can be re-used. However, nobody can approach the audacity of George Romney, the head of American Motors Corporation, who, when facing the economic recession of 1958, decided to recycle an entire automobile!

The plan was simple: dust off the tooling of the 1955 Nash Rambler 2-door sedan, slightly modify it to open up the rear wheel arches and simplify the hood design, add a mesh grille and a little chrome – and launch it as the new 1958 Rambler American. The experts said it wouldn't work, after all the Nash design actually dated back to 1950, but Romney had spotted a niche in the market for a US-built small car with a thrifty six cylinder engine at a rock-bottom price.

The Rambler American sold well, helping to put AMC in profit at a time when the competition was suffering losses. And, as frugal as the owners of the little car he was so enthusiastic about, Romney wasn't about to spend any more money on building the American than he had to. It continued almost unchanged until 1960, with increasing sales, establishing itself as the leader in the compact car sector at minimal cost.

Although he was careful to control spending, Romney appreciated that this virtual monopoly couldn't last forever. The popular

Volkswagen Beetle continued to dominate the import market, and the Studebaker Lark was the first American-made competition to arrive in '59. When GM, Ford and Chrysler entered the fray in 1960, George Romney knew it was time to act in order to protect AMC's hard-won customer base. Even then, chief stylist Edmund Anderson was only allowed to re-skin the ancient bodyshell.

Given these constraints, Anderson's achievement is remarkable. While the inner panels remained untouched and so the interior dimensions of the American were as before, the overall length was reduced by 5.2 inches and the width by over 3 inches giving a far neater package. Measurements aside, the squarer body now had a more modern Sixties shape and could stand alongside the competition without looking old fashioned.

The distinctive trapezium-shaped grille, sharp leading edge "brow" that flowed into a gradually flaring side indent and simple round tail lights weren't to everyone's taste. Critics have called Anderson's design "boxy and truncated" while supporters claim the car is "a little jewel". One feature that Anderson couldn't alter was the high beltline level, but this wasn't significantly detrimental. George Romney described the car as having "modern, enduring style".

Most customers were happy with the new look and, once again, AMC defied the detractors and sold 136,000 Americans in 1961, and a total of 370,600 cars, lifting the Rambler to an unprecedented third place in the charts behind Chevrolet and Ford (albeit a long way behind, by something like a million units!). Styling was no doubt important, but the American was more about economy than

Above: Restyled and modern-looking, the Rambler American for '61 was smaller than the '60 models, but kept its spacious interior. The 2-door sedan was the most popular model.

Left: The Rambler American 4-door station wagon was added to the model line-up for '61. Wagons could be ordered in all three trim levels: DeLuxe, Super and Custom.

Right: The 2-door convertible only came as a top-of-the-range Custom and was the most attractive of the American range. It was economical at under $2400 and 13,000 were sold.

prestige and AMC used the slogan "the top resale value among the low-priced cars year after year" to reinstate that Rambler buyers could expect a better price than other owners when trading in their car for a new model.

By 1961, there was more choice for the Rambler American driver too. From the one model "plain Jane" 2-door sedan of '58, the range now featured three levels of trim – DeLuxe, Super and Custom – with a variety of bodystyles, including a new 4-door station wagon and a convertible. The top of the line Customs were also equipped with a modern overhead valve in-line six cylinder engine that produced 125bhp. This powerplant was available as a $59.50 optional extra on the lower specification models, otherwise you got the 90 horsepower antique flathead six. Both engines displaced 195 cu.in.

Not only was there a wider choice of models, Rambler American owners could now also specify extra creature comforts from an options list. You could jazz up the exterior with two-tone paint for $15.95, add front and rear DeLuxe foam rubber seat cushions at $19.90, or the ultimate has to be the Airliner Recliner Seats that folded down into Twin Travel Beds. If it was ease of driving you were after, there was the lever control Flash-O-Matic automatic transmission ($165), power steering ($72) and power brakes ($38). The most expensive add-on was undoubtedly air conditioning, which came with a heavy-duty cooling system and a hefty price tag of $359

Below: The Dodge Dart Phoenix was restyled for '61 with curious rear tapering tail fins whereas the rest of the industry was getting rid of fins. It was completely revamped for '62.

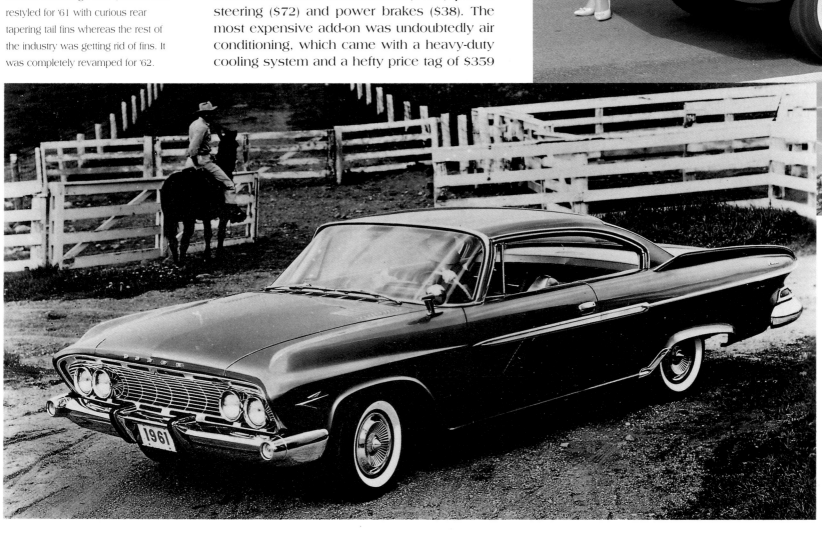

– almost 20% of the cost of the cheapest American model.

The best seller was the DeLuxe 2-door sedan at $1845, which compared favorably against $2230 for a basic Chevrolet, and 28,555 were produced. But if the Rambler buyer got carried away and opted for too many extras, the "cheap little compact" soon became as expensive as a full-size automobile. Mind you, the Chevy salesman wasn't going to let a customer out of the showroom without ordering a few extras either, so the price differential was pretty much maintained at the end of the day.

Away from the motor industry, President Kennedy was promising to put a man on the moon before the end of the decade and Alan Shepard became the first American in space on July 21st. Less memorable was the failure of the CIA-orchestrated Bay of Pigs invasion of Cuba in April, and the decision to send 400 Green Berets to Vietnam. Also on the downside was an attack on the Freedom Riders in Alabama during a protest over segregation on buses, and a spate of airliner hijackings.

But there were plenty of winners to celebrate in 1961 too. Phil Hill became the first American to win the Formula One World Championship driving a Ferrari, A. J. Foyt took the chequered flag at the Indianapolis 500 (the first of four victories at The Brickyard) and Marvin Panch won the NASCAR Daytona 500 in a Pontiac. To compare the success of a cheap, compact, family car from an independent manufacturer based in Kenosha, Wisconsin with some of the great names in motor racing might seem a bit presumptuous. However, finishing third for Rambler was an amazing achievement given their limited resources. By beating the might of Detroit, AMC, George Romney, Ed Anderson and the Rambler American deserve to be included in the list of winners in '61.

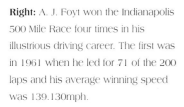

Above: New to the compact market, the Oldsmobile F-85 came with 215 cu.in. aluminum V8 Rockette engine that produced 155bhp in standard form and 185bhp with the power pack option of a four-barrel carb, high compression heads and dual exhausts.

Right: A. J. Foyt won the Indianapolis 500 Mile Race four times in his illustrious driving career. The first was in 1961 when he led for 71 of the 200 laps and his average winning speed was 139.130mph.

1962

By 1962, the Studebaker-Packard Corporation was in serious trouble and the end of the road was in sight for the once-proud names of two long-established marques who had merged in 1954. In fact, the last cars bearing the Packard badge were actually produced in 1958 and Packard was dropped from the company name in '62, marking the final sad ending of a history of building fine automobiles that stretched back to 1899.

But Studebaker still struggled on, and even in their death throes, they managed to produce some rather remarkable automobiles. Probably the most notable of these was the Grand Turismo Hawk which was a face-lift of a design dating back to 1956 (the '56 was actually a revamp of the body shell first introduced in '53!). The updated design was produced at record speed and with very little expenditure. The car enjoyed a favorable reception and its success can be gauged by the comments in Motor Trend who called it: "A bold new approach to luxury and power – a man's car all the way". Technical Editor Jim Wright described the response from other drivers by saying: "If the amount of interest generated in and around the Los Angeles area is any indication of what Studebaker-Packard can expect throughout the rest of the country, then we'd say their new Grand Turismo Hawk is definitely 'in'."

Other motoring magazines were equally supportive. Car Life stated: "In some ways, it was the most appealing car we've driven this year... It's very much the kind of car we'd be happy to own." Wheels magazine described it as "quick and handsome", while the reporter for Modern Motor magazine said about it: "...it's all motor-car, in the best sense of the term. The most advanced by far that I've driven." Judging from these reviews it would seem that Studebaker had created a triumph in spite of the prevailing doom, much in the same way as a conjuror pulls a rabbit from a hat. Unfortunately, Studebaker needed some magic of a more powerful kind to survive, and even the most skilled illusionist couldn't hide the enormity of the task facing the company which eventually folded in 1966 – after closing the South Bend, Indiana factory and moving its operations to Canada toward the end of 1963.

The foundations of the GT Hawk were laid by the studio of extrovert stylist Raymond

Loewy (whose long association with Studebaker resulted in some wonderful automobiles) with the new 1953 models which included the graceful Starliner hardtop and Starlight coupe – the work of designer Bob Bourke, assisted by Holden Koto. The Loewy

Below: The Bonneville was still the top Pontiac series for '62 and the design grew a little longer as the marque showed an improvement in sales. On March 14th 1962, the 75 millionth GM car built was a Bonneville convertible.

Above: Studebaker's Grand Turismo Hawk is the result of designer Brooks Stevens amalgamating several familiar styling themes taken from rival prestige cars and turning them into a highly effective design.

studio also carried out the update for the '56 Hawk range, but this was to be a final collaboration and thereafter the relationship ended. The main reason for the split was one of cost. Strapped for cash, Studebaker couldn't justify the expense of the high-profile Loewy organization and started to seek out cheaper freelance designers.

The task of rejuvenating the Hawk was given to Brooks Stevens who has, over the years, accumulated many great designs in his portfolio, but who is probably remembered most often as the man behind the Excalibur automobile.

At a time when the development of a new model (or even a relatively straightforward face-lift) was usually measured in years rather than months, Stevens worked something of a miracle in just a few weeks. The first hand-built example was put together at his

Milwaukee workshop in June '61 and finished versions were in front of Studebaker dealers by September! It was a truly remarkable turn round.

What Stevens did in essence was to take a good, if out-dated, design, refine it and add a quality of style and distinction that befitted a classic grand tourer. The rakish Fifties tail fins were quickly consigned to the rubbish bin to be replaced with far neater items, and the external re-skinning presented a flatter, more elegant body. Efforts were then concentrated on the roof section creating a squared-off, formal appearance which many people said was a direct copy of a Thunderbird, although Studebaker claimed it had been derived from the Packard Predictor concept car which had been built six years earlier.

Other styling elements that Stevens used to good advantage were altering the grille

Above: Described as the "projectile look" by designer William Boyer, the third generation Thunderbird had a pointed nose, razor-sharp lines, round tail lights with vanes in the trim and abbreviated fins. This was a land-locked missile, thanks to a 300 horsepower 390 cu.in. V8 under the hood.

Below: In an attempt to boost flagging sales, the Sport Fury model was announced four months after the rest of the Plymouth line. Available either as a hardtop sedan or convertible, and loaded with extras, the public still continued to shun Exner's designs and Plymouth sales plummeted.

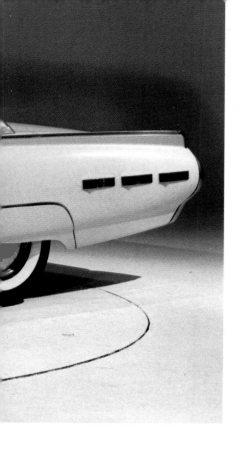

which gave it a slight resemblance to the Mercedes (Studebaker was then the distributor for Mercedes-Benz cars) and adding a chrome strip along the belt line on top of the fenders which ran the whole length of the car in much the same manner as the Lincoln Continental.

This device of using styling features to bring an association with recognized upmarket automobiles could have been a disaster, but Brooks Stevens managed to bring all the elements together and made it work beautifully. The only item that looks out of place is the false, stick-on trunk lid "grille" which was used to disguise a virtually unchanged component. This was deleted for the '64 GT Hawks (the final in the series) and there's no doubt the smooth uncluttered panel works far better. The trunk lid apart, the decoration on the car is minimal and chrome trim is used in a restrained manner.

To back up the looks, a true GT needed some respectable performance, and here the Studebaker was able to take care of itself pretty well. The 289 cu.in. V8 engine might have been a touch on the heavy side for its capacity, but it was durable and, in standard form, it put out 210 horsepower which was sufficient to give a top speed over 100mph. For those who wanted to do some really "grand" touring, there was also a 225bhp option which included a four barrel carburetor and dual exhausts and, together with the four-speed manual transmission (three-speed was

standard and automatic was also an option), this provided sufficient performance for one magazine to label the Hawk "an enthusiast's car". In subsequent years there were even more powerful choices available, including a supercharged Avanti engine, but these are rare finds today.

Another highlight for Studebaker in 1962 was having the Lark Daytona chosen as the pace car for the Indianapolis 500 and, while Raymond Loewy's radical new Avanti would also provide the company with plenty of publicity, it couldn't halt Studebaker's slide into obscurity.

Studebaker's woes paled into insignificance compared to those facing the nation. The Cuban missile crisis saw JFK and Russian premier Kruschev bring the world to the brink of another war in October. Thankfully, everybody was able to breath a sigh of relief when the Soviet government backed down from the confrontation. A tragedy that was mourned by red-blooded men around the globe was the death of Marilyn Monroe on August 5th – an event that is still shrouded in intrigue today.

There was no such mystery over the demise of Studebaker. Poor management decisions following World War Two, inadequate investment for the future and difficulties with controlling the work force all contributed to the downfall. Even so, the company built some excellent automobiles and the Grand Turismo Hawk rates as one of the best.

Below: Introduced to counter the popularity of the Ford Falcon, the Chevy II arrived in '62. The no-nonsense economy model could be had with a four cylinder engine in the cheapest form, but a mid-level 300 like this 4-door sedan also came with choice of a 194 cu.in. straight six. Sales of all Chevy II variants reached over 326,000 in the first year.

1963

During the life of the Corvette there have been some highs and lows along the way, but ten years after the model's first introduction came one of the truly great ones – the 1963 Sting Ray.

What makes an automobile great? In this instance it is a perfect combination of styling and performance. And the plaudits for achieving such an outstanding example of the automotive art must go to two men – Bill Mitchell and Zora Arkus-Duntov. Mitchell, as vice president in charge of design for General Motors, regarded the Corvette (and especially the Sting Ray) as very much his own baby, even to the extent of warning off other in-house designers from attempting to come up with new ideas for styling the car. Engineer extraordinaire and successful racing driver, Arkus-Duntov was responsible for transforming the Corvette's handling and giving it the horsepower needed to perform.

Motor racing played a key role in the evolution of the '63 Sting Ray. To begin with, Bill Mitchell acquired the test vehicle from the abandoned Super Sport project (a factory-backed program developing a Corvette for endurance racing) and had Larry Shinoda design an open-top body for it. Shinoda took a lot of his inspiration from the Q-Corvette, an experimental rear-engined sports car that was the creation of Bob McLean – the designer who had laid out the very first Corvette. Mitchell christened his racer the Stingray

Special and got Dr Dick Thompson to drive it in the SCCA C-Modified class where it quickly proved to be a winner, taking the championship. At the end of the 1960 season, Mitchell decided he couldn't afford to keep funding the race car and so sold it back to GM, where it was rebuilt as a show vehicle.

By that time, progress was well in hand for what would become the sensational 1963 Corvette. Mitchell made no secret of his love for knife-edged styling and used it to great effect on the final production design which also incorporated the "triple hump" feature seen on the fenders and hood of the Stingray racer and Mako Shark concept car. But while the '63 Sting Ray was just about all new from the ground up (apart from engines and transmissions) Mitchell was careful to ensure some continuity of styling from the preceding years, and to this end had introduced the "duck-tail" rear on the '61 Corvette to give everyone the chance to get used to the theme.

At the Sting Ray's leading edge, the aggressive appearance was emphasized by the use of hidden headlights – the first time this device had been seen on a Chevrolet, and not used on any other US car since the 1942 DeSoto – but it was the rear window in the fastback boat-tail coupe model that would prove to be the most contentious feature of all. Bill Mitchell was adamant that the split rear window should stay and he argued long and hard to get his way saying "…if you take that off, you might as well forget the whole thing." Mitchell won the day, but criticisms in the press about restricted rear visibility and further pressure from people like Zora Arkus-Duntov saw the central spine removed for the '64 models, giving the 1963 Sting Ray a

Right: A split rear window was only used on '63 Corvettes, and has become an identifying feature of the model. But the boat-tail fastback coupe was much more than a styling exercise, giving superb performance. However, the duck-tail rear was a carryover from the preceeding model years to give continuity.

Below right: Hidden head lights were a rare concept on US-built cars in the Sixties, this Chevy sports car being the first since the 1942 DeSoto to use the idea. The knife-edge Corvette styling was a sensation at the time, and is as striking today as it ever was.

Below: After the disasters of '62, Plymouth models like this Sport Fury Hardtop had a hasty redesign but, although sales improved, the Chrysler division was still well behind Chevrolet and Ford in the race for customers. Top of the range Sport Fury models came with bucket seats, central console, de luxe steering wheel and interior trim, and special wheel covers.

146

unique identifying feature and instantly turning it into a highly collectible item.

It has to be said, however, that some '63 models subsequently had their split rear windows replaced with a one-piece window and, after the 1964 model became available, Chevy dealers even offered a factory conversion – which immediately destroyed the car's value and it's certain that many Corvette owners today regret their actions.

As well as the split windows, Bill Mitchell also included several other non-functional styling ideas that met with disapproval and were dropped in '64. Dummy metal inserts in the hood copied lift-reducing vents used on Mitchell's Stingray race car and were deleted,

and fake ventilation outlets behind the coupe door pillars were replaced with functional grilles. Another feature removed after the first year was the stainless steel trim on the windshield pillar.

But apart from stunning looks, a sports car is all about performance and the Sting Ray had that too, thanks to Zora Arkus-Duntov who stated: "For the first time I now have a Corvette I can be proud to drive in Europe." His starting point was a simple, but highly effective, steel ladder chassis that proved so good it remained in Corvette production for 20 years with only minor alterations. Coupled to the channel section frame was an all-round independent suspension system which

Above: Raymond Loewy's Avanti was a desperate attempt to rescue the image of the ailing Studebaker marque by creating a grand tourer in the classic mode.

Right: Avanti was powered by a supercharged 289 cu.in. V8 and gave a 0-60mph time of 7.3 seconds, but the 2-door coupe with fiber glass body suffered from production problems. European styling didn't appeal to everyone and less than 5,000 were built by Studebaker although Avanti continued under different owners.

endowed the Sting Ray with a cornering capability equal to the best of the competition. The most ingenious part of the suspension was the rear set-up which used a single transverse leaf spring and rugged, almost crude, construction to provide the equivalent of more sophisticated designs at a fraction of the cost.

Getting around corners efficiently is all very well, but the speed on the straights linking those bends is mighty important to the sports car enthusiast too. Once again, Arkus-Duntov had worked his magic and the Sting Ray could be had with horsepower aplenty. Standard was the 250bhp 327 cu.in. V8, but you could also order the optional 300bhp L75 version, 340bhp L76 or the fuel injected, 11.25:1 compression, Duntov cammed L84 specification which produced 360bhp at 6000 rpm. Car Life tested a 300bhp version with automatic transmission and recorded a 0-60mph time of 7.2 seconds which they reckoned compared favorably to the 5.9 secs achieved by Road & Track driving a 360bhp/4-speed manual car. Top speed was put at 130mph – fast enough for most, but there was potential for quite a bit more if needed.

From the start of the Sixties, Corvette sales had begun to climb from an average of around ten thousand a year, but so well was

the '63 Sting Ray received that a second shift was taken on at the St Louis assembly plant to fulfil the growing demand. Even so, there was a two month waiting list, and buyers could expect to pay the full sticker price as dealers weren't interested in offering any discounts. At the end of the model year, the Corvette Sting Ray had sold more than 21,500 units, split almost equally between the coupe and roadster, and virtually doubled the 1961 sales.

However, one event overshadowed 1963 and anyone who was alive back then can remember exactly where they were and what they were doing on November 22nd when they heard the news that president John F. Kennedy had been assassinated in Dallas, Texas. Measured against such a tragedy, all other events pale into insignificance. It is impossible to say how differently things might have turned out had Kennedy not been shot, but the dynamic spirit of America survived and, in some small way, the Chevrolet Corvette can be viewed as a symbol of US determination to overcome all obstacles and produce something that is as good as anything manufactured elsewhere in the world – but at a price affordable by the majority. All Corvettes are great, but some are better than others and the '63 Sting Ray is undoubtedly one of the greatest.

Above: Typical of Sixties factory-supported drag racing machines is this Ford Galaxie 300 Club Coupe. Powered by a 427 cu.in. engine with 11.5:1 compression ratio and twin Holley four-barrel carbs that pumped out well in excess of a conservatively rated 425bhp, these machines were the terrors of the tarmac quarter mile.

1964

The first Ford Mustang is an automotive phenomenon that it would seem impossible ever to repeat. Just imagine suggesting that a new, but completely conventionally-engineered automobile based on an existing compact, economy model would sell nearly half a million in the first year and go on to set a trend affecting manufacturers for the next thirty years or more. Yet that's exactly what happened in 1964.

Ford certainly pressed all the right buttons with the Mustang, but had the good fortune to get some unintentional help from rivals Chevrolet and Plymouth. The Ford Falcon – introduced as a 1960 model following the success of the Rambler American and the demand for a cheap compact car – proved an immediate winner, taking up most of the spare production facilities left over from the Edsel debacle. The Chevy Corvair and Plymouth Valiant also entered this market sector, but a combination of radical rear-engined configuration (Corvair) and quirky styling (Valiant) gave the Falcon a distinct advantage. Ford were also able to utilize the compact's underpinnings in such a way that was impossible for Chevrolet to do with the Corvair, and although Plymouth had a similar idea with the Valiant-based Barracuda their offering lacked the Mustang's glamor.

As the US economy started to improve in the early Sixties, customers began to ask for better performance from the smaller models and the auto makers were happy to oblige – after all, luxury and extra horsepower options meant more dollars! But though the uprated Falcon Futura Sprint and Corvair Monza models were acceptable, they didn't really satisfy the younger generation of affluent car buyers' demands for a true sporty compact that was just that little bit different from the usual run-of-the-mill Detroit products.

Whenever the history of how the Mustang came into being is discussed, one name always gets top billing – Lee Iacocca. Described as "The Father of the Mustang", Iacocca had the energy and foresight to get the project underway and the determination to see it through, even when Ford's top management kept refusing to approve the construction of such a car. Several Ford concept cars came under consideration for inspiration when the design parameters were being set,

but the most logical choice seemed to be for a snappy little four-seater based on the Falcon platform.

Before this, Ford stylists John Najjar and Jim Sipple came up with a sleek two-seater roadster body that was dubbed Mustang I and, powered by mid-mounted V4 engine, was demonstrated by Dan Gurney at the 1962 US Grand Prix. Although an interesting vehicle which contained several styling cues that would find their way onto the production

Above: The Ford Mustang established a new class of automobile called the "pony car" and set sales records that are unlikely to be bettered. The early ragtop has a 260 cu.in. V8 which gave lively performance in a smart, reasonably-priced package.

version, Mustang I didn't really fulfil the requirement that Iacocca and his committee had laid down. Further design development work was needed and this culminated in an internal competition between the Ford Studio, Corporate Advance studio and Lincoln-Mercury. The proposal presented by the Ford Studio team headed by Joe Oros, Gail Halderman and David Ash, was unanimously chosen as the winning design, and this was eventually turned into a running prototype in

Above: Elwood Engel had replaced Virgil Exner as head of styling at Chrysler and one of his first designs was the '64 Imperial Crown which carried several styling cues from the Lincoln which Engel had worked on. Similarities of slab sides, sharp-edged fender lines and even the hint of the Continental's spare wheel hump in the trunk lid are apparent.

Below: The Chevrolet El Camino re-appeared after a four year gap, but was now based on the mid-sized Chevelle, rather than a full-size car as before. Dubbed a "personal pickup" by Chevy, the '64 El Camino came in two trim levels, with six cylinder or V8 engines and a wide variety of passenger car type options.

1963 called Mustang II which is generally acknowledged as being the forerunner of the production Mustang.

Iacocca set the launch date for the Mustang as April 17th 1964 at the New York World's Fair but, just over a month before that, the Motor City press were allowed an "accidental" sneak preview when Walter Ford (Henry Ford II's nephew) drove a pre-production Mustang convertible to a lunchtime meeting in downtown Detroit. The photos were quickly circulated to other magazines and newspapers and the corporate publicity machine swung into action to keep interest at a fever pitch until the official debut.

Pandemonium broke out wherever the Mustang went on sale and there are many stories of the chaos caused by Ford's new car – some of which had little foundation in fact, but it all added to the hype. Not that the Mustang needed much hyping – dealers couldn't write up the orders quick enough and it took only four months to reach 100,000

sales – a total which had been earlier forecast for the first twelve months! Demand was at such a pitch that the Ford assembly plants at Dearborn, Michigan and San Jose, California were working flat out to keep pace and, early in the summer, a third plant at Metuchen, New Jersey was brought on-stream and ran around the clock pumping out Mustangs.

While it was clear that the Ford designers had created a car totally in tune with the times, a major contribution to the Mustang's popularity was the extraordinarily low base price of $2,368 f.o.b. Detroit for the coupe model. This was the price that Ford pushed in its advertisements, but it only bought the standard straight six engine with three-speed manual transmission – the big news was the lightweight V8 available at extra cost.

And it was the extensive options list that provided the opportunity for each owner to transform a docile, if stylish, standard specification automobile into anything from a grand tourer in the classic mold to a tire-shredding

hot rod. This incredible variety of choice was even more surprising when you remember that, underneath the bodywork, most of the mechanical components came directly from the old Falcon. It also meant that although the Mustang was aimed at younger drivers, ownership was opened up to anyone – there was no such thing as a typical Mustang buyer, they ranged from eighteen to eighty, and the car was equally welcome at the country club, fashionable restaurant and church as at the local drive-in or drag strip. That remains as true today as it ever was.

What achieved such a broad spectrum of appeal? There's no doubt that the classic sports car "long-hood, short-deck" proportions set the right image, and the Mustang name evoked connotations of everything positive about the American way of life — but most of all it was about timing. The Mustang was simply the right car at the right time. Arriving at the precise moment when speed and performance were becoming major selling points

as the "muscle car" era took off, even parked by the side of the road, a Mustang had the look of motion that Lee Iacocca had appreciated when he first saw the clay mock-up presented by Joe Oros.

The term "pony car" came to represent a new class of automobile, which Ford called "the family man's sports car" in its adverts, and one that remains in use even today. And although the Mustang is still in production, the "Mustang generation" (a description first used by a California real estate developer in a sales brochure promoting apartments for young singles) belongs to the Sixties.

The Beatles brought pandemonium to the streets of New York when they arrived in February, and Lyndon Johnson's landslide victory to retain the presidency over Barry Goldwater in November was seen as a vote to unify the nation but, in 1964, the one thing that all generations of Americans were united about was their love of the Mustang and the streets and highways were filled with them.

Above: Shoehorning a large engine into a small car and giving it a fancy name cribbed from an Italian sports car might not sound too inspiring, but John Z. Delorean had the right idea when he came up with the Pontiac GTO. Actually a Tempest Le Mans option, the GTO spec included 389 cu.in. engine, floor shifter, uprated shocks and dual exhausts and is regarded as the first of the Sixties "muscle cars".

Below: Introduced as a '63 model, the Buick Riviera had only small detail changes for 1964 and remained a stunning sports luxury car in the classic mold. The most expensive Buick, it was both fast and elegant, thanks to 425 cu.in. engine and crisp lines from stylist Bill Mitchell.

1965

Speed was on people's minds in 1965, particularly towards the end of the year. On 12th November, Bob Summers pushed the world land speed record for wheel-driven vehicles to 409.277mph at Bonneville, making his Goldenrod car the fastest on earth. Three days later, on the 15th, Craig Breedlove and his jet-powered Spirit of America took the world record for non-wheel-driven cars to 600.601mph, a phenomenal achievement.

Meanwhile, safety campaigner Ralph Nader, was also looking at speed when he published his book "Unsafe at any Speed", which condemned, among others, Chevrolet's Corvair. But following in the hoofbeats of Ford's new Mustang, many manufacturers were scrambling to produce sporty models of their own to cash-in on the market for speed among car buyers of all ages. Since few were able to introduce completely new sporty cars like the Mustang, most updated more mundane-looking intermediates from their existing ranges.

At Plymouth, 1965 saw the demise of the Sport Fury as the company's leading sporty model. The car had grown in size and had more luxurious appointments than before, something that did not really fit into the sporty image. To replace it, the company introduced the Belvedere Satellite, which came with a V8 engine as standard, albeit a small one, and had lots of performance options depending on how much muscle the buyer wanted to flex – and, of course, on his pocketbook.

Before 1965, the Belvedere name was used on Plymouth's middle-priced, full-size cars, and it was more an indication of the level of trim and equipment than a model in its own right. In '65, however, the Belvedere series comprised a trio of intermediate-size automobiles, based on a 116 inch wheelbase. The three cars varied in their standard level of equipment and trim, being known as Belvedere I, Belvedere II and Belvedere Satellite, the last being the top of the range aimed at buyers who wanted a bit more performance than the norm.

Belvedere I and II models could be supplied with 225 cu.in. ohv, six cylinder engines or 273 cu.in. 180 horsepower V8s as standard, backed by a three-speed manual transmission with the option of a Torqueflite automatic. Body styles available comprised 2- and 4-

Left: The Rambler Marlin was AMC's attempt at producing a pony car to match Ford's Mustang. It had sleek fastback styling that was decidedly stylish, but its standard 232 cu.in. six cylinder engine let it down.

Left and below: The Satellite was the sporty version of Plymouth's Belvedere intermediate and it came with enough engine and performance equipment options to turn it into a real tire-burner. In standard form, it came in hardtop and convertible models equipped with a 273 cu.in. V8 and three-speed. However, the buyer could choose between five optional engines, ranging from a 318 to the mighty 426 Hemi backed by a four-speed.

door sedans, 4-door station wagons, a 2-door hardtop coupe and a 2-door convertible. The Belvedere Satellite, however, only came with the V8 as standard, and in hardtop and convertible form. From the outset, it was given a sporty image, with front bucket seats, a center console and full wheel covers that incorporated center spinners. The hardtop also received all-vinyl trim. Emphasizing the performance look of the car, the rear fenders featured a row of louvers, while bright rocker panel moldings were also fitted.

The big news for the Satellite, however, was the range of engine options listed. These began with the 230 horsepower Commando 318 cu.in. V8 equipped with a two-barrel carburetor, followed by a similarly-equipped 361 cu.in. Commando engine that developed 265 horsepower, and a 383 with a four-barrel carburetor that was good for 330 horsepower. If that wasn't enough, the buyer could specify the 426-S wedge-head V8, which displaced

155

Above: Ford's big Galaxie was completely updated for 1965, having new body styling on a new perimeter frame with coil-spring suspension front and rear. The squared-off styling included vertically-stacked dual head lights and matching tail lights. This 4-door sedan was one of several body styles offered.

426 cu.in. and had a four-barrel and developed 365 horsepower. The amount these engines added to the cost of the car ranged from $31 to $545, depending on the engine. For those with deep pockets and an urge to burn rubber, however, there was the 425 horsepower, 426 cu.in. Hemi engine with dual four-barrel carburetors and a price tag of either $1150 or $1800. This included the cost of a four-speed manual transmission. There were two prices because the engines were retrofitted at the factory, and the higher figure applied to cars that had originally been equipped with automatic transmission. The same arrangement applied to the wedge-head engines, with two prices being quoted. Given that the base price of a Satellite 2-door hardtop was $2612, the hemi represented a substantial investment and, in truth, these engines were really intended for competition use.

Although the four-speed came as standard with the 426 engines, it could also be specified with the 361 and 383 engines, while a positive-traction rear axle was also available for an extra $39. Other performance options included a choice of rear axle ratios (3.23 or 2.93:1) and a tachometer.

Not many Satellites had the monster 426 wedge-head or hemi engines. Most buyers opted for the more tractable 383 V8, which

had power and torque aplenty and was much more user-friendly on the street. But the big engines, particularly the Hemis, were in keeping with Chrysler's interest in NASCAR and drag racing. In the former, the Hemi would be fitted to full-sized Dodges and Plymouths run on tracks of over a mile in length, while on shorter tracks, Dodge Coronets and Plymouth Belvederes would use it. In drag racing, too, the Hemi-engined Belvedere was legendary, being campaigned by the likes of Ronnie Sox and Buddy Martin and the "Drag-On-Lady" Shirley Shahan, who used it to set a National S/SA record of 127.30mph with an elapsed time of 11.21 seconds. Such was the company's interest, that they produced an altered-wheelbase drag package for Dodge and Plymouth automobiles so that they could compete in the NHRA Factory Experimental class.

The actual body styling of the Belvedere models had been carried over from the previous year, when it had been common to all intermediate Plymouths. For 1965, it was changed by replacing the previous dual head lights with single lights, while the grille was given a cruciform trim with mesh background.

The sporting image of the Satellite that resulted from the company's NASCAR and drag racing activities, plus the undoubted performance of the car, helped boost sales and just over 25,000 of the 1965 models were built, most of them hardtops (only 1,860 convertibles left the factory). The car continued with this image for some time, and in 1966 was restyled with a swoopier roofline and more slab-sided contours. The big news for that year, however, would be a more refined 426 Hemi engine that was intended for street use. The Street Hemi had cast-iron cylinder heads rather than aluminum (although these were available as an option), while the inlet manifold was aluminum rather than magnesium. A wilder cam was available, and although compression was down to 10.25:1 from 12.5:1, output was still 425 horsepower. With this came a Sure-Grip axle, whether a four-speed or Torqueflite automatic was fitted.

The Street Hemi turned out to be a real winner, offering tractability as well as high performance. Car and Driver said that the car offered the "best combination of brute performance and tractable street manners" that they had ever come across. In their test of the car, they recorded a 0-60mph time of 5.3 seconds, with a 13.8 second quarter mile time and terminal speed of 104mph. Stopping such a projectile needed substantial brakes, of course, and while front discs were not an option, 11 inch police-specification drums were.

Although it never looked particularly like a muscle car, Plymouth's Belvedere Satellite was definitely a force to be reckoned with. It would go on in this vein, eventually spawning the famed GTX and Road Runner.

Above: Oldsmobile's 4-4-2 muscle package had appeared as an option on the F85/Cutlass series in 1964. Then the figures had stood for four-barrel carburetor, four-speed manual transmission and dual exhausts. For 1965, the package gained a 400 cu.in. engine in place of the previous 330 cu.in. unit. So they now stood for 400 cu.in., four-barrel carb and dual exhausts.

Below: The Galaxie hardtop was a particularly good looking car with sharp styling. In total there were six main series of Galaxie, giving 17 models. Engines comprised six and five V8s, the most powerful producing 431 horsepower.

1966

If you're involved with the decision making process at the upper end of management for a division of a large auto corporation, it is accepted that there will be a great deal of give and take. In all probability, you do not wield enough influence to insist on your division being able to produce a brand new model from the ground up – you have to share the basic corporate platforms with the other divisions and make as many alterations as is allowed within the constraints of the budget available. In this respect, Chrysler in the Sixties was no different from the many other large companies leading the automobile industry.

However, just once in a while, restrictions such as these engender creativity which produces something very special and the 1966 Dodge Charger is an outstanding example of what the art of compromise can achieve.

Around the mid-1960s, the fastback body style enjoyed a period of popularity as the result of the rest of the auto industry rushing to come up with their own versions of the ultra-successful Ford Mustang. Dodge were offered the opportunity to share the Plymouth Barracuda platform with this in mind but, instead, they decided to go their own route and use the larger Coronet model as a basis for an entry into the burgeoning muscle car market.

The leading lights at Dodge behind this policy were product planner Burt Bouwkamp and stylist William Brownlie – both newcomers to the division and both self-confessed performance car buffs who simply loved the work they were doing.

Even so, the merits of the Sixties fastback are hard to define from a practical point of view. Rear seat passengers had restricted headroom and minimal leg space, the large area of glass created a greenhouse effect causing the interior to heat up rapidly in the sunshine and, to cap it all, luggage space was abysmal. On the plus side of course, the fastback Charger does look great. Even when it is standing still, it seems ready to spring into tire-blistering action – and, when talking about muscle cars, that counts for a whole lot more than how much shopping can be accommodated in the trunk or the niceties of passenger comfort.

The starting point for the Charger actually came about almost by chance rather than

being attributed to part of some grand corporate marketing strategy. Facing the lack of an attention-grabbing exhibit for an auto show in the summer of '65, Bouwkamp asked Brownlie to come up with an idea for a show car that could not only be built quickly, but at minimal cost. It was a tall order, but the

Below: The Comet Cyclone GT adopted the Ford Fairlane body shell and had a 335 horsepower, 390 cu.in. engine plus twin hood scoops, heavy duty suspension and dual exhausts. Only 2,158 GT convertibles were built in '66, making it highly-collectible.

Above: Hidden head lights and a full-width grille give the Dodge Charger an aggressive look, matched by ground-shaking acceleration thanks to the brutal horsepower of a 426 cu.in. Hemi engine. This was the car described as "...the hot new leader of the Dodge Rebellion".

Above left: The finely-sculpted Charger has a sweeping fastback roof line which was popular in the late Sixties, but the Dodge hardtop coupe was one of the most attractive versions. This model sold 37,300 in its first year but this halved in '67 when the body style remained virtually unchanged.

designer rose to the challenge and suggested putting a fastback roof on the popular Dodge Coronet model. Following Brownlie's specifications, a 2-door hardtop was speedily modified and readied for the show.

Dubbed "Charger II" (Dodge had used the Charger name before on another show car a year or two previously), this car was not, as is often supposed, intended as an official prototype for a proposed new model but was simply created as a last minute showpiece. However, public reaction to the fastback was so enthusiastic that plans were immediately rushed through to put the Charger into production.

Brownlie's show car had, naturally enough for something designed to attract attention, several rather exaggerated styling features and it was deemed necessary to trim these excesses back for the version intended for sale to the public. Nevertheless, the production Charger retained all the good points of the original concept. The sloping fastback roof remained unaltered, and the full-width

Above: The arrival of the Ford Bronco Sports Utility pickup showed a new market was opening up for a 4x4 leisure vehicle that could "go nearly anywhere and do nearly anything". "Neither a car nor a truck, but a vehicle which combines the best of both worlds", the Bronco closely resembled the International Scout which had debuted in '61.

tail lights were incorporated in a flat rear panel with the slab-sided fenders neatly squared off at the back and a razor-sharp top edge picked out with a bright metal strip.

But it was the front end that provided the most radical departure from the show car's original appearance. In place of the simple grille with five thin horizontal bars and single rectangular head lights, the Charger presented a blank face made up of fine vertical lines interrupted only by the round medallion in the center. Hidden head lights, another Sixties styling fad, were in vogue and the use of them on the Dodge represented the first time that they had been seen on a Chrysler Corporation car since the 1942 DeSoto. When turned on, the four round head lights rotated into view but there was an override switch allowing the lights to be left exposed without being on. This feature was a clever Dodge engineer's solution to the problem of head light mechanisms being frozen shut in harsh winter conditions, which had blighted this feature on other makes.

The interior of the Charger, especially the dashboard and instrument layout, was taken almost directly from the show car and used unaltered, providing one of the most comprehensive packages on offer at that time. Elsewhere, it was luxury all the way with deep plush carpets and foam-padded bucket seats, plus a fake wood rimmed steering wheel as the final touch. In addition, the rear seats folded flat to give increased carrying capacity but, without a full hatchback, it didn't really help much on a practical level.

Because of the low budget allocated, the Charger II show car had a meek 318 cu.in. V8 under the hood, but the majority of '66 Chargers were ordered with the 325 horsepower 383 cu.in. engine. Thus equipped, the

Right: The Oldsmobile Toronado was an ingenious piece of engineering which successfully used a big V8 engine mounted in the conventional position with a front-wheel-drive system. The first front-wheel-drive American car since the Thirties Cord, it was designed to give sports car handling on a roomy six passenger sedan, and proved its worth when Nick Sanborn won the stock car class of Pikes Peak hill climb in '66 driving one.

hefty fastback could reach 60mph in eight seconds, cover the quarter mile in sixteen at over 90mph and run on up to reach a 120mph top speed.

But for the serious performance devotee, there was only one powerplant – the mighty 426 Hemi. Fed by dual Carter AFB four barrels and rated by the factory at a very conservative 425bhp, this engine gave the Charger a 0-60mph time of six seconds, and quarter miles in the 13 second bracket. As befits a road-going race car, underneath, everything about the Hemi Charger was heavy duty, from the vented four-pot front disc brakes, massive torsion bars and anti-roll bar to extra rear springs and Dana 60 axle.

There was one thing that the Hemi Charger didn't come with – a factory warranty. Instead, there was a bright yellow sticker which stated: "This car is equipped with a 426 cu.in. engine (and other special equipment). This car is intended for use in supervised acceleration trials and is not intended for highway or general passenger car use. Accordingly, THIS VEHICLE IS SOLD "AS IS", and the warranty coverage does not apply."

Driving a Hemi-powered Dodge Charger could undoubtedly be a very exciting experi-

ence, but the year's ultimate piece of steering must go to astronaut Neil Armstrong who, when piloting the Gemini 8 space craft, performed the first docking manoeuvre and described it as "Just like parking a car". Other people on the way up were Ronald Reagan who was elected as Governor of California, and The Monkees pop group who were launched into the limelight through a madcap television series. Also riding high were the hems of women's' dresses and skirts across the nation as high fashion saw the mini skirt become all the rage.

Dodge used the success of the Charger to launch a campaign called "the Dodge Rebellion" and the new fastback sold well on the back of some heavy media promotion and race-winning results, but the '67 body looked identical and sales halved in the following year. A completely new shape arrived in 1968, making the first Dodge Charger very much a child of its time.

1966 was the year that civil rights movement leader Stokely Carmichael brought the term "Black Power" into the forefront of the American political debate, but for an automotive enthusiast it was the year of "Hemi Power" and the Dodge Charger.

Below: This was to be the final year for Studebaker, with cars like this Daytona 2-door Sports Sedan being built in Hamilton, Ontario, Canada. Only 2,321 Daytona models were built (out of a total of just under 9,000 units) before production was closed down in March 1966 and the Studebaker name disappeared.

1967

Coming second to Ford is something that Chevrolet has never liked and, when the Mustang proved to be such a runaway success in 1964, the heat was on to find a way of redressing the balance. Chevy supporters will tell you that there were all manner of reasons why the GM division didn't have an equivalent to Ford's pony car – the Corvair Monza was selling well, they had too many different models already on offer – but the plain fact of the matter is that Ford had got there first, and so it was down to Chevy to play catch up.

Wisely, the Chevy hierarchy appreciated that arriving second in the market place meant that they had to produce more than just a Mustang clone – a new model had to be perceived as something better. Ford and Chevrolet fans will debate forever about which is best, but there is no doubt that the Camaro provided a more than adequate riposte to the Mustang and, even if it did take until 1977 to outsell the Ford, the Chevy Camaro was definitely here to stay.

Taking advantage of the example provided by Ford, Chevy abandoned the rear-engined layout of the Corvair and returned to the conventional front engine, rear-wheel-drive arrangement for their new car. Henry Haga was put in charge of the styling and, in addition to the Mustang, his influences came from a clandestine 1962 project by Chevy design director Irwin Rybicki that used a Chevy II as the base. Certain similarities can also be seen with the Corvair Monza. Due to a management reshuffle, David R. Hollis took over as chief designer and, after four months intensive work, in December 1964, a full size clay model was constructed and photographed against a Mustang for comparison.

Initially, the "Chevy Mustang" project was given the Experimental Project code number XP-836. Later on it got christened the "F-Car" (the "F" supposedly referring to Ford), and subsequently carried the name Panther, which many assumed would be the final model name. However, General Motors was locked in a battle with Ralph Nader and his safety crusaders during this period, and it was decided that using the Panther name was too provocative, and so a search began for an alternative. Chevrolet's head man, Elliot M. "Pete" Estes reckoned that the name should start with a "C" and, for a while, the name "Chevette" was under consideration,

Above: The Chevy Camaro was available with everything from an economical six cylinder up to one of the hottest small block V8s on the market. The basic version here has simple round head lights and turn signal lamps mounted in the grille. Only 2-door hardtop coupe and convertible body styles were offered, with the Camaro roof line being such that a fastback was not deemed necessary.

Left: The Camaro Z-28 was the hottest option, intended mainly for Trans Am racing, and included a special 302 cu.in. V8 rated at 290 horsepower although it was actually capable of well over 425bhp in racing trim. Only 602 Z-28 specification cars were built in 1967.

New Camaro BY CHEVROLET

Left: The Super Sport 350 Camaro has bumble bee stripes around the nose and a 350 cu.in. V8, but the grille with electrically operated head light covers actually forms part of the Rally Sport option which were often ordered together to make a stunning combination.

163

but merchandising manager Bob Lund and vice president Ed Rollert searched through Spanish and French dictionaries and picked out the word Camaro in one of them. Estes liked the name and it was announced to the press in June '66, well in advance of the car itself being previewed. Chevy publicists said Camaro translated from French as "comrade" or "pal", but other researchers noted that in Spanish it could be interpreted as a type of shrimp or even "loose bowel movement" – but the fuss soon died down and the name became established as quintessentially Chevrolet.

When the Camaro was announced, on September 29th 1966, it was immediately apparent that Chevrolet's designers had taken the Mustang concept to heart and yet had added their own distinctive ideas. Where the Mustang's body lines were straight and aggressive, the Camaro's were curved and flowed ("fluidity" was a term used a lot by GM's designers) and the Chevy shape had been the subject of wind tunnel testing to prove its superior aerodynamic performance.

But it wasn't only in the bodywork design that the Chevy differed from the Ford. The basic understructure consisted of a front sub-frame attached to a unitary bodyshell, instead of the complete unitized construction used on the Mustang. In many ways this configuration gave the Camaro an advantage and, because the front chassis could be isolated from the rest of the body with rubber bushings, the ride quality was improved. In addition, the design had better space utilization, improving the room allocated for rear seat passengers and the trunk capacity.

But despite these improvements, the Chevy Camaro was not without its teething problems. While the attractive 2-door coupe body could happily rival both that of the Mustang notchback and fastback models, the convertible suffered from body flexing, door sagging and rattles all of which required fixing. Also, the single leaf Mono-Plate rear springs used were okay with the base six cylinder engine and Powerglide automatic transmission, but the more powerful V8 cars suffered from axle tramp and all '67 Camaros

Above: The Cadillac Eldorado used a front-wheel-drive system and combined roadability with superb styling. The Cadillac 472 cu.in. V8 could give 125mph top speed and nearly 18,000 were sold in '67.

Below: Pontiac adapted a Chevrolet Camaro bodyshell for their entry into the pony car market in '67 with the Firebird. Pontiac engines and firmer suspension gave improved handling.

would bottom out on the rear suspension with alarming ease.

Like the Mustang, the Camaro could be specified with any number of additional options selected from a huge list. In fact, the list was so comprehensive and so complicated that it was suggested that few people really understood all the available possibilities. Apart from the bewildering array of engines, transmissions, colors, interior trim and special packages on offer for the standard specification car, the potential Camaro owner could also select from some serious high performance options – notably the Super Sport (SS), Rally Sport (RS) and the now legendary Z-28.

Once you got into the SS and RS models (which, to add to the muddle, could also be combined together on one car), the Camaro came with hidden head lights and a special paint stripe around the nose plus various other items. But the "bumble bee" stripe proved to be so popular that it was quickly made available on any Camaro model. Then, when the big block V8s were introduced, the SS package came as a mandatory part of the deal. Confusing? You bet!

Despite this apparent minefield of choice, nearly 65% of the 220,906 '67 Camaros produced were base model V8 Sport Coupes and there can be few people who would argue that this was, indeed, a pretty shrewd selection for just about any form of motoring. Whether cruising down to the corner drive-thru

burger joint or high speed touring cross-country on the Interstate, it was all the same and the Chevy proved a match for the Mustang in just about every department.

"Long-awaited and much-speculated, the youthful Chevrolet Camaro has arrived on the domestic automotive scene with a fine pedigree and high promise", wrote Car Life magazine in October 1966, continuing: "Though a follower in a field pioneered by others, the Camaro nonetheless seems exciting in looks and performance, is particularly well-suited to its intended market and will be sold and serviced by the world's largest dealer body". This emphasis on youth and excitement reminds us that these were indeed the heady days of the Sixties – 1967 being the so-called "Summer of Love" when everything went psychedelic and the Monterey Pop Festival heralded the hippie culture taking over San Francisco.

There were plenty of dark clouds in the purple haze, what with continuing Vietnam War protests, race riots in the Motor City of Detroit and the tragic deaths of three astronauts – Virgil Grissom, Edward White and Roger Chaffee – when their Apollo spacecraft caught fire on the launchpad at Cape Canaveral. Despite the harrowing events of this year, however, memories of '67 will, for most people, be of a highly colorful and supercharged period that welcomed the arrival of the Camaro as a small part of the more positive trends in society.

Above: The Mercury Cougar was a cousin of the Ford Mustang and a de luxe entry in the pony car market, priced about $200 higher, but with a 200bhp 289 cu.in. V8 as the base engine. Riding on a 111 inch wheelbase (3 inches longer than the Mustang), the Cougar was easily identified thanks to its grille: 123,672 were sold in '67 – its debut year.

1968

By 1968, the United States was heavily involved in the Vietnam war. The conflict had cost billions of dollars and, subsequently, American taxpayers were saddled with a 10% rise in their taxes. Harder to swallow still, was the number of American lives lost, and there seemed no end in sight. Despite putting out peace feelers in the previous year, the North Vietnamese together with the Vietcong, launched a massive new offensive at the end of January, during the sacred Tet new year holiday, penetrating the grounds of the US embassy in Saigon. In fact, the Tet offensive was a desperate gamble for the North Vietnamese, who had suffered considerable losses in both men and equipment as a result of US bombing, particularly in the north of the country, but it paid dividends. Stung by the speed and success of the attack, and by the ever-growing peace protests at home, President Lyndon B. Johnson ordered a halt to the bombing of North Vietnam. The demoralized Johnson did not seek re-election later that year and was succeeded by Republican Richard Nixon, whose Presidency was to be less than trouble-free.

Along with the relentless grind of the Vietnam war, there was more bad news that year: civil rights activist Martin Luther King was assassinated, and attorney general Robert Kennedy shared his fate a short time after. The one bright piece of news was that Apollo 8 became the first spacecraft to orbit the moon, paving the way for a manned landing in the following year.

In Detroit, the car makers were still caught up in the muscle car business. All had at least one horse in the race, which was fast becoming a contest to see who could cram in the biggest engine and out-accelerate the rest. Straight-line performance was the main criterion and, in the process, handling, braking, ride, build quality and levels of trim often left a lot to be desired.

For 1968, Buick's entry in the pony car wars was the Gran Sport, which became a model in its own right that year. Prior to that, the Gran Sport had been an option package that was available on the company's 115 inch wheelbase compact model, the Skylark.

When Ford announced the Mustang in 1964, they had caught everyone on the hop. A mad scrambling ensued among the other manufacturers to produce a comparable car and take advantage of the lucrative pony car market. Unable to develop a completely new model in time, Buick reworked the relatively mundane Skylark in 1965, offering a package that included a 400 cu.in. big-block V8 engine, three-speed manual transmission, uprated chassis, rear axle and suspension, wide wheels and revised exterior trim. Despite the prissy Skylark name, the Gran Sport offered some genuine muscle, cranking out a 0-60mph time of six seconds, while on the drag strip it ran the quarter mile in 14.7 seconds with a terminal speed of 100mph.

Right: AMC's pony car was the AMX. Featuring unibody construction, the standard car had a 290 cu.in. V8, but 343 and 390 cu.in. V8s were among the options.

Below: The Buick Gran Sport had GM's new "B" body with its distinctive sweeping side molding and had big-block 340 and 400 cu.in. engines that delivered astounding acceleration.

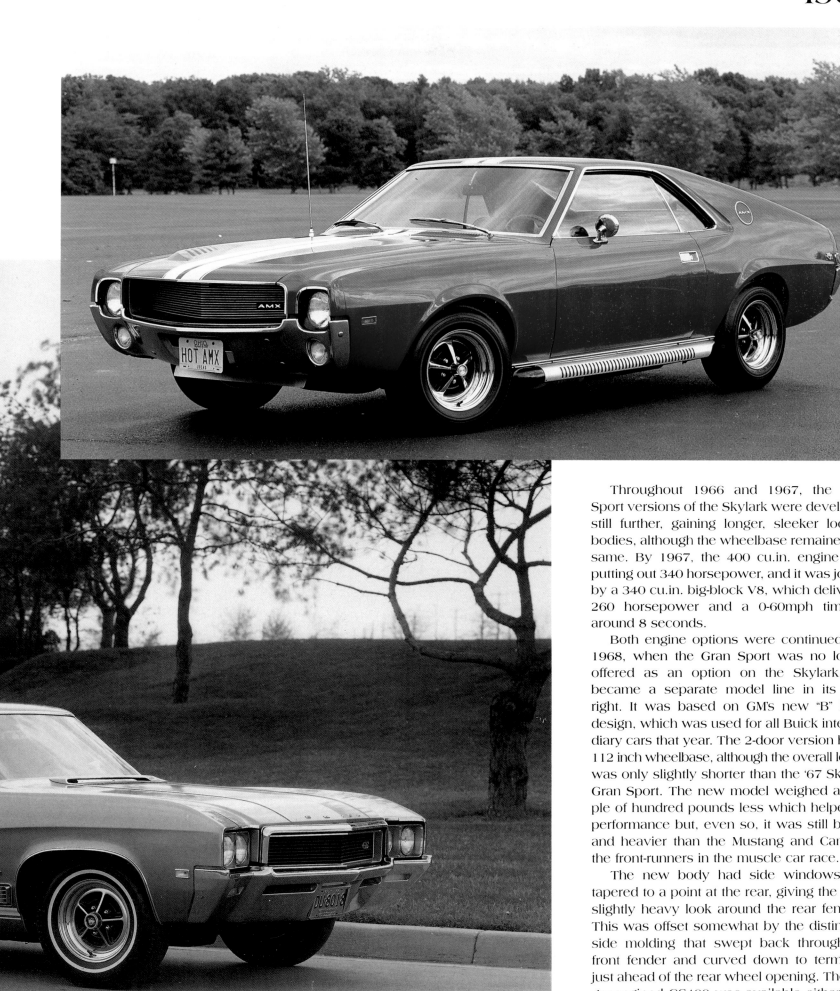

Throughout 1966 and 1967, the Gran Sport versions of the Skylark were developed still further, gaining longer, sleeker looking bodies, although the wheelbase remained the same. By 1967, the 400 cu.in. engine was putting out 340 horsepower, and it was joined by a 340 cu.in. big-block V8, which delivered 260 horsepower and a 0-60mph time of around 8 seconds.

Both engine options were continued into 1968, when the Gran Sport was no longer offered as an option on the Skylark, but became a separate model line in its own right. It was based on GM's new "B" body design, which was used for all Buick intermediary cars that year. The 2-door version had a 112 inch wheelbase, although the overall length was only slightly shorter than the '67 Skylark Gran Sport. The new model weighed a couple of hundred pounds less which helped its performance but, even so, it was still bigger and heavier than the Mustang and Camaro, the front-runners in the muscle car race.

The new body had side windows that tapered to a point at the rear, giving the car a slightly heavy look around the rear fenders. This was offset somewhat by the distinctive side molding that swept back through the front fender and curved down to terminate just ahead of the rear wheel opening. The bigger-engined GS400 was available either as a hardtop or a convertible, while the GS340 was available as a hardtop only. Bench seats were standard in all versions (front buckets

167

were optional), but both GS models could only be considered four seaters. Like most muscle cars, they sacrificed refinement for performance, and this was not helped by the poor quality of build prevalent at the time.

Among the options offered with the Gran Sport was a choice of transmissions. As standard, the car came with a three-speed manual with floor shifter, but the buyer could order a four-speed manual transmission instead, or an automatic.

Like so many other muscle cars, the Gran Sport was not a comfortable car for long-distance touring. With its stiff suspension, the car's ride left a lot to be desired, while either big-block engine made it nose heavy with a detrimental effect on the handling.

Where the Gran Sport really scored was in its blistering straight-line performance; for anyone who wanted to burn rubber, neither the GS400 nor GS340 would let them down. The gutsy, big-block Buick V8s churned out gobs of horsepower, but the gearing was such that top speed was only about 110-115mph, and they would only get about 11-14 miles on a gallon of gas.

The major problem was that, even as early as 1968, all the manufacturers were chasing a muscle car market that was already beginning to disappear. The hullabaloo that followed the launch of the Mustang had died down and emissions controls were beginning to hamper the cars, increasingly emasculating their performance. Interest was on the wane and the potential buyers were starting to look for more traditional features in a car. Although the bubble had not burst, it was beginning to deflate. In 1965, when Buick introduced the first of the Gran Sport options

on the Skylark series, they sold over 69,000 examples of the sporty car. Despite the new body styling, for 1968 the sales of the Gran Sport totaled only 21,514.

Although sales figures continued to fall, Buick persevered with the Gran Sport, keeping it in production until 1972 but, by that time, it had returned to being a version of the compact Skylark. Along the way, it received trim changes, a 455 cu.in. engine in place of the original 400 cu.in. unit, and a 350 cu.in. V8 instead of the 340. Other options included hot camshafts, revised valve trains, positraction rear ends and dual exhaust systems. For the hot rodder who wanted to drag it out, these may have been very welcome, but they were not enough to keep the breed alive.

1969

As the sixties came to a close, America still found itself enmeshed in the Vietnam war, although the number of US troops there was being reduced and efforts were being made towards the Vietnamization of the war by providing material and air support to the indigenous forces of South Vietnam. The anti-war rallies continued and home-coming troops who had served in South East Asia often returned to find that they were looked upon with disgust by many of their peers, despite the fact that most of them had been drafted. Later in 1969, news of the massacre of innocent civilians in the village of My Lai by American troops stirred up the anti-war sentiment all the more.

It was a year of mourning, not just for the thousands who had died in Vietnam, but also for one of America's great heroes of the twentieth century. On 28 March, the country was shocked by news that Dwight D. Eisenhower, former President and Commander in Chief of the Allied forces in Europe during World War II, had died.

If many Americans were not proud of what was being done in their name in Vietnam, all had reason to be proud of their country's achievements in space. Following successful orbital missions to the moon, NASA carried out a successful landing in July, and Neil Armstrong became the first man to set foot on its dusty surface, quoting the now immortal phrase: "One small step for man; one giant leap for mankind".

The auto industry, however, took a slightly shorter step that year, with new car sales being a little below those of the previous year. It was not the easiest of times for manufacturers. With increasing pressure to improve the exhaust emissions and safety aspects of cars, production expenses increased. By this time, the industry's flirtation with the compact had just about come to an end, and the future seemed to lie with intermediate-sized cars. Some, however, continued to build big cars, among them Chrysler – a company that was rarely known for styling innovation, although they often led the field in engineering. The real luxury models in Chrysler's line-up came from the company's Imperial division which, for many years, had sought to compete with Cadillac for the prestige end of the market. For 1969, the Imperial range comprised of 2-

and 4-door hardtops and a 4-door sedan. In addition, a custom-built limousine was also available to special order.

Imperial had been a name associated with Chrysler for decades but, until the mid Fifties, it had simply been applied to the most luxurious models sold under the Chrysler badge. The company built long wheelbase sedans

Below: Based on a 127 inch wheelbase, the 1969 Imperial was a very big car. Compared to previous Imperials, the cars sold well, even though they were obviously Chryslers under the skin.

Above: Both 4-door and 2-door hard-top Imperials were built, together with a 2-door sedan. Although originally intended to compete with Cadillac, the Imperials could never quite make the grade.

Right: For 1969, Lincoln's Continental Mark III remained pretty much unchanged from when it was announced in 1968. The 2-door body was based on the Ford Thunderbird, although this was by no means obvious. It was given a Rolls-Royce-like grille, which was flanked by fold-away head lights. Powered by a 365 horsepower, 460 cu.in. V8, the Mark III was an instant success.

Below right: Many manufacturers were still playing the pony car game in 1969. Chevrolet not only had the Camaro, but also the Chevelle SS 396, a high-performance version of its standard Chevelle intermediate-sized automobile.

Below: Oldsmobile's 4-4-2 was another tire-burning muscle car that shared the GM "B" body with Buick's Gran Sport, among others. Powered by a 400 cu.in. V8, the car was offered with a range of options, including forced-air induction and a variety of rear axle ratios.

and limousines as well as other luxury models under the Custom Imperial and Crown Imperial names. However, these were obviously Chryslers and could be associated with more mundane company products. It was not good marketing for a company that wanted to do well in the luxury market, dominated by Cadillac.

If Imperial was to make it, the image of the cars had to improve; they needed to be less obviously part of the Chrysler empire, with a mystique of their own. As a result, in 1955, a separate Imperial division was formed and a new range of Imperials launched. Sadly, one of the new cars – the 2-door hardtop – looked very similar to the Chrysler C300, a popular high-performance automobile that had done well in competition. This undoubtedly affected the sales of the Imperial range, but even so their total sales doubled compared to the year before.

However, Imperial had become established as a maker of luxury cars, and the name became more familiar with buyers. Until the mid Sixties, many Imperials were designed by Virgil Exner, who had some quirky ideas of what made a good-looking luxury car. As with most other automobiles of the late Fifties, Imperials grew fins that became ever-larger with each new model. Unfortunately, because the company had relatively limited resources, new models appeared less frequently than those of other manufacturers and, towards the end of each model run, the cars were beginning to look decidedly dated. This is particularly true of the '62 models which had outlandish fins at a time when all other manufacturers had dropped the idea. Lights were another of Exner's foibles. Wanting to give his designs the classic look of Thirties automobiles, he incorporated freestanding head lights and tail lights that looked as though they had been stuck on as an afterthought. If nothing else, Imperials were unique in appearance.

Exner was eventually replaced by Elwood Engel, who had worked at Ford, and he brought a considerable degree of Lincoln influence to the '64 Imperials, which were big slab-sided automobiles. From this point on, Imperials tended to reflect design trends within the industry, rather than setting standards of their own.

However, with falling sales, costs had to be cut so, for 1967, the Imperials used the basic Chrysler New Yorker body shell, although different front and rear end treatments gave it a distinctive appearance. It was a unibody design fitted with a 440 cu.in. V8 that developed 350 horsepower and was backed by a three-speed TorqueFlite auto-matic transmission; this was the same drivetrain that had been used in previous models. Imperials were back where they started, being uprated versions of existing Chrysler models. Things would stay that way until all production ceased in 1975.

Although featuring a completely new 127 inch wheelbase body, when the '69 Imperial models were unveiled, the similarity with the New Yorker was even more pronounced. The body had gently rounded sides and was referred to by Chrysler as having "fuselage styling". The drivetrain was the same as that used previously, while power steering and brakes were standard equipment. Two series of Imperial were built: Crown and LeBaron. The latter was the more luxurious of the two and was available on both hardtop models, while Crown versions of all three body styles were available.

There is no doubt that all the Imperial models were luxury cars – for Chryslers. But the company had slipped out of the market they had long wanted to be a part of. Moreover, they would never return.

Despite its obvious Chrysler parentage, the 1969 Imperial sold well compared to previous years. In total, just over 22,000 examples were built; the last time sales had been above 20,000 was at the launch of the new 1964 model. Sadly, that was the highpoint for, thereafter, sales dropped quite alarmingly (by almost 50% in 1970 and 1971). Minor changes were made until 1974 when, again, it shared the latest New Yorker body shell. By this time, Imperial no longer existed as a separate division of Chrysler. However, the oil crisis of 1973 had sounded the death knell for big gas guzzlers and, after 1975, production of Imperials was brought to a halt.

1970

Imagine taking a chainsaw and hacking off the back of a compact family sedan to produce a sub-compact model, giving it a whacky name and introducing it on April 1st! Bizarre? Well, this was how economy-minded American Motors Corporation (formerly Rambler) chose to compete with the rising tide of imported four cylinder small cars and, at the same time, beat the Ford Pinto and Chevy Vega models into the market by six months.

Well, maybe the chainsaw was a bit of an exaggeration but, by reducing the wheelbase of the Hornet by a foot and using most of the

same front panels, interior and underpinnings, AMC were able to bring the Gremlin to production with incredibly cheap tooling costs. Not that the original Hornet hadn't been designed by Dick Teague with some ingenious money-saving features to begin with. For a start, front and rear bumpers were interchangeable, 2- and 4-door models shared the same roof pressing, and costly versions like the 2-door hardtop and convertible were deliberately omitted from the line up.

Chopping the Hornet off short to make the Gremlin wasn't a new idea for AMC – they'd done just the same thing a couple of years earlier with their Javelin pony car in order to produce the AMX two-seater sports coupe. And, to keep the Gremlin base price to a bare minimum, it was introduced as a two-seater with just a rubber mat in place of the rear seat. Actually setting the price caused AMC a few headaches as, being the first of the US

Left: The basic Gremlin was pretty spartan, but options could be added such as a roof rack, body stripes, wheel covers and whitewall tires – and this also helped AMC profitability. The hatch-style opening rear window was only used on four-passenger models. 28,500 Gremlins were sold by the end of 1970.

Right: The Gremlin was identical to the larger Hornet model from the doors forward, saving on tooling costs. It used the same six cylinder engines, transmissions, and suspension components to further reduce production expenditure. The wheelbase of 96 inches was a foot shorter than on the Hornet, but the Gremlin was only 3.5 inches longer than the VW Beetle.

manufacturers into the sub-compact field with a home-produced car, they didn't have any competitors to gauge their offering against. In the end, the cheapest Gremlin was set at just $1,879 – aimed right at the P.O.E. price of the cheapest Volkswagen Beetle.

But, exactly as anticipated by AMC chairman Roy Chapin, very few of these base model Gremlins were sold and, instead, customers went for the four-seaters with extra options which all helped to push the price (and profitability) up. Advertising for the Gremlin emphasized the fun aspect of the car, with its practicality and economy being an added bonus. This struck a chord with many of the younger generation who also liked the fact that the quirky styling didn't appeal to their parents.

Market research had shown AMC that there was a youthful market with considerable purchasing power for cars like the Gremlin, and predicted that the demand for new small cars would exceed the combined sales of standard size, medium and luxury

cars in a few years time. Their studies showed that a typical Gremlin purchaser would be in his or her early 30s and have an annual income of $10,000. A high percentage would be women, and single people would make up a quarter of the total. It was forecast that by 1975, persons under 34 years of age would buy 40% of all cars in the USA and 60% of all compact and sub-compact models.

At the press launch in Palm Springs in February 1970, president of American Motors, William V. Luneburg, announced the car with the following statement: "The Gremlin is the first domestic car specifically designed to meet the foreign car challenge and halt its domination of a sizable segment of the American market. We believe the reason more and more buyers have turned to imports is that they did not have an acceptable alternative among US cars for the combination of features they were seeking in a smaller car. The Gremlin includes not only the desirable features of import-size cars but also provides the handling and roadability charac-

Above: The Ford Maverick was billed as the "first car of the '70s at 1960s prices". The Economy model was introduced on April 17 1969, exactly five years after that other popular equine Ford, the Mustang. Powered by a 170 cu.in. six cylinder, the Maverick proved to be in such demand that it remained unchanged throughout the 1970 model year too. With a 103 inch wheelbase, it wasn't really in the sub-compact class, but still sold over 450,000 units in its first full year.

teristics most US buyers want."

Although all the other sub-compact cars had four cylinder engines, this was one item that AMC couldn't offer and the Gremlin came with a 128hp, 199 cu.in. straight six as standard (a 232 cu.in. 145hp six was optional). Somehow this didn't matter in 1970, as quite a few people looking at a smaller car for the first time were a bit unsure about durability and found a smooth, torquey six more comfortable than a high-revving four. In following years the Gremlin also acquired a 304 cu.in. V8 under the hood – some were even drag raced with the 401 cu.in. engine – and it wasn't until towards the end of its life in '77 that a four cylinder VW/Audi powerplant was used.

Another advantage that the Gremlin had over the smaller imports was the list of extra convenience equipment that could be specified. For American drivers unused to manual gear shifting, the Shift-Command automatic transmission was a plus, as were the power brakes and Variable-Ratio power steering and, of course, there was also air conditioning. For the more performance-orientated, there was a handling package including

heavy-duty springs and shock absorbers and front sway bar, and Twin-Grip limited slip differential and special axle ratios. All told, more than forty items were available as factory installed options and, naturally, many dealer installed accessories could be had as well.

Offbeat it may have been, but the Gremlin fitted right in with the needs of AMC in the early 1970s to create positive media coverage, promoting interest and thereby sales. After the Rambler name had been dropped, Roy Chapin faced an uphill battle to establish the identity of American Motors with the public and there's little doubt that bringing out such an unusual shape as the Gremlin on April Fool's Day guaranteed widespread publicity. Chapin was nobody's fool, however, and the Gremlin sold well – over 671,000 between 1970 and '78 – with just an occasional face-lift, making millions of dollars for the company and helping it to survive.

The design of the Hornet/Gremlin can be traced back to the experimental Cavalier unveiled in 1966. On a nationwide tour, the Cavalier generated a good response, particularly for the use of interchangeable components – for instance, left front and right rear fenders were identical. Several styling cues from the Cavalier were carried through to the

Gremlin, including wide wrap-around grille, flared wheel arches and ventless side windows. Another associated design study was the AMX/GT, a two-passenger show car using the abrupt chopped-back configuration.

Something like a Gremlin is bound to be full of surprises, but how many people would have described it as a 2-door sedan? That's what AMC chose to call it, saying quite straight-faced, "Diminutive in an automotive sense, it is not a scaled-down version of any American Motors passenger car". But the point they were trying to make was that the extra width inside the Gremlin gave more shoulder and hip room when compared to any other import in the sub-compact category.

The Gremlin might have looked weird to some, but generally it could be relied upon to raise a smile for daring to be different in what were difficult times. 1970 saw four students killed at Kent State University in Ohio by the National Guard during an anti-war demonstration and women protesters marching for equal rights in New York – unrest was everywhere. Maybe only AMC could have gotten away with the Gremlin but, coming from a year when smiles were a bit thin on the ground, the sawn-off little car deserves to be remembered with affection.

Above: The Plymouth Road Runner Superbird was developed in a wind tunnel to win NASCAR stock car races, and qualifying speeds of over 190mph were recorded at the super speedways like Daytona and Talladega. Around 1,935 road-going versions were sold, although prices were heavily discounted towards the end as demand didn't live up to Plymouth's expectations. When powered by the legendary 426 cu.in. Hemi V8 engine, this is an awesome street machine!

1971

Following the success of the Disneyland theme park in Anaheim, California, 1971 saw the opening of the much larger Disneyworld in Orlando, Florida. No doubt, this was well received by kids all over the States, but young people in their late teens would probably have been more interested in the fact that henceforth, from age 18, they would be eligible to vote in all political elections.

People in the news that year included the boxer Muhammed Ali, who was cleared of draft dodging after his earlier refusal to join the army, which inevitably would have resulted in him being sent to Vietnam. The pardon allowed him to resume his successful boxing career. One person who would not receive a pardon, however, was cult leader Charles Manson, who was sentenced to death for the murder of actress Sharon Tate in 1969.

Meanwhile, NASA had sent men to the moon again, but this time they had taken along a set of wheels for exploring the lunar landscape. The Lunar Rover gave the astronauts mobility, but it was not the swoopy space vehicle of science fiction. Little more than a bare frame, it was fitted with a pair of seats and equipped with special wire-mesh wheels driven by electric motors. However, it did the job, although it had to be left on the moon, as the astronauts' spacecraft did not have the capacity to bring it home.

Back on earth, towards the end of the year, GM recalled a record 6.7 million cars to rectify a problem with faulty engine mounts. It was not their most memorable achievement that year, but one that was more notable was the launch of Buick's new Riviera. Although not to everyone's taste, the Riviera had eye-catching styling teamed with luxurious appointments and plenty of power.

By 1971, the styling of most Detroit products was becoming a little subdued compared to previous years. While many of the designs were good, few could be considered head-turners. One automobile that did turn heads, however, was the Riviera.

Since the introduction of the 1963 Riviera, GM's design department, under the leadership of Bill Mitchell, had been turning out elegant designs for Buick's personal luxury car. All stood apart from the run-of-the-mill models, and the '71 was the most outstanding yet. Mitchell had been the driving force behind a number of unique designs for GM, among

them the 1963 Corvette Sting Ray, which shared one important feature with the new Riviera: the tapering, boat-tail shape of the rear roof and deck. It was this aspect of the design that caused the most comment from magazine road testers and potential buyers alike. Some loved it; others hated it.

Like the earlier models of the Riviera, the 1971 version was a 2-door hardtop coupe. It was based on a new 122 inch wheelbase perimeter frame, which was longer than the previous model by some 3 inches. This helped emphasize the long, sleek shape with overtones of an earlier era that designer Jerry Hirshberg had penned for the body. When viewed from the side, the line of the front

Above: The rakish looking '71 Riviera was slightly longer than its predecessor, which helped the sleek design. However, the optional vinyl-covered roof detracted from the design somewhat, breaking up the clean lines.

Right: The most distinctive feature of the design was the tapering boat-tail, which projected beyond the rear deck and was mirrored by the shape of the inset bumper. The trunk lid incorporated louvers on '71 models, but these were dropped for 1972, as was the boat-tail itself in 1973.

fender swept back and curved gently downward, continuing well into the door, the top of which also ran downward slightly towards the rear. Immediately behind the door, the line kicked up quite sharply to match the prominent curve of the rear fender. The shape of the latter was quite pronounced, bulging slightly out of the body, much like the rear fenders of a Forties Roadmaster although, in this case, the fender itself tapered downward to the rear.

The overall effect was that of the classic "leaping cat" shape found in so many sports and luxury cars of the Forties and Fifties. The line through the fender and door emulated the outstretched front limbs, while the rear fender echoed the powerful haunches, pushing the body forwards. It was unlike anything offered by any other US manufacturer at the time.

On top of this traditional outline, was the unique roof treatment. From the steeply raked windshield, the roof curved down to the tapering boat-tail. This swept across the deck and came to a rounded point that projected out from the rear of the car. This projection was emphasized by the trailing edge of the trunk lid, which tapered inwards slightly from the rear fenders in a shallow V-shape. The inset bumper mirrored the shape of the trunk lid and boat-tail. The latter was flanked by two narrow rectangular tail lights, while the license plate was sent into the bumper on the left side.

The roof treatment was pure '64-67 Sting Ray, only wider. The rear window was of the

Left: The Pinto was Ford's 1971 entry into the small-car field. With a wheelbase of 94 inches, there was a choice of four cylinder engines with capacities of 98 cu.in. and 122 cu.in.

Below right: Dodge was still selling muscle in 1971, but this would be the last year for the mighty Charger R/T. Equipped with heavy-duty suspension and brakes, it was powered by the 440 cu.in. Magnum V8.

Below: In 1971, GMC offered a dual-purpose truck, the Sprint. This used the same body as Chevrolet's El Camino, with which it would have competed for sales.

same shape, while the same raised molding ran down the center of the roof and continued beyond the rear window, right down to the tip of the tail. The window itself proved a problem in more ways than one. Because of its size and position, it had to be specially tempered to withstand the stresses imposed on the body when the car was driven over extremely harsh road surfaces. This resulted in a slight distortion of its optical qualities. Moreover, the large area of glass exposed to the sun could turn the interior into an oven quite rapidly, so air conditioning was an essential option for cars that were destined to spend their lives in the sunnier states.

At the front, dual head lights flanked a simple grille of horizontal bars, while rectangular parking lights were incorporated in the lower bumper. Although there was a degree of peaking to the hood, the front end styling was somewhat subdued compared to the rear.

Inside, the car was well trimmed with the dashboard taking on a dual binnacle form, with the triple-faceted instrument panel designed so that all controls and instruments directly faced the driver. Despite the car's size, the interior was not exactly roomy, and it would be better described as a 2+2 rather than a full four seater.

Mechanically, the new Riviera was similar to its predecessor, having coil spring suspension all round and front disc brakes as standard (although these had been an option of the previous model). However, the earlier models had demonstrated quite poor handling, so Buick engineers redesigned the suspension to good effect, producing a car that

rode and cornered well. Moreover, the Riviera could be ordered with the Max Trac option – a computer-controlled system that prevented wheelspin and fish-tailing under hard acceleration on slippery surfaces by restricting the amount of power fed to the rear end.

Only two models of Riviera were available: the base version and the Gran Sport (GS). Both were powered by a 455 cu.in. V8, which produced 315 horsepower in the former. However, the engine of the latter was equipped with a modified carburetor, a different camshaft and other bits and pieces that bumped output to 345 horsepower. In both cases, the engine was backed by a Turbo 400 three-speed automatic transmission, with a choice of column- or console-mounted shifter.

With the big 455 engine, the Riviera offered performance to match its striking looks, and was capable of reaching 60mph in around 9 seconds with a top speed in the region of 125mph. However, with such a large engine and weighing in at 4500 pounds, gas mileage was not outstanding, although the car had never been designed with economy in mind. It had a very well-defined, but limited, market, being aimed at junior executive types who were moving up the income scale and wanted to say to all and sundry: "Look at me; I'm going places". Within this market, the Riviera sold well and steadily. It continued in production through 1972 and 1973, although in the latter year it lost the distinctive boat-tail and received the federal "5mph" bumpers. After that came another restyle, but never again would the Riviera be the head turner or performer it once was.

1972

With every move geared towards securing a second term in The White House, in many respects, 1972 was a good year for Richard Nixon. He got off to a good start by visiting communist China in February; in June he had a summit meeting with Soviet leader Brezhnev; and he was pulling American troops out of Vietnam. However, in June an event came to light that no doubt Nixon would have preferred to remain secret. It was some time before he was directly linked to the burglary of the Democratic Party's head-quarters in Washington's Watergate Building and, in the meantime, he had won the sought-after second term. But when the truth came out, he had no choice but to go. Out of office and in disgrace, he retired to his home in California, but eventually he would bounce back, becoming a venerated elder statesman.

The Watergate scandal would rumble on for many months but, in September, Americans had good reason to be proud. At the Munich Olympics, swimmer Mark Spitz picked up seven gold medals, while Bobby Fischer beat Boris Spassky to become the first American World Chess Champion.

In Detroit, Ford's Lincoln division also had reason to be proud. 1972 saw the launch of the Continental Mark IV, replacing the Mark III, which had been introduced in 1968 as a direct competitor to the Cadillac Eldorado, achieving immediate success. The luxurious 2-door coupe was originally conceived on the 117 inch wheelbase Ford Thunderbird perimeter frame. It utilized portions of the T-bird's cowl and roof but, for the Mark IV, designer Wes Dahlberg used a new 120.4 inch perimeter frame, giving the car greater luxury and style.

The styling clues of the Mark III were continued, however: the classic long hood/short deck proportions; the prominent Rolls-Royce-like grille flanked by fold-away head lights; the tall, slightly rounded sides; the low roofline and Continental spare hump in the trunk lid. Because of the longer wheelbase, the rear roof pillar was wider than that of the Mark III, and Dahlberg put this to good use by incorporating an oval opera window.

In keeping with the car's luxury status, the Mark IV was richly upholstered with "loose cushion" seats, while the dashboard was designed to reduce injury in an accident. As an added safety feature, sturdy crash rails were incorporated in the doors.

Top & above: The Lincoln Continental Mark IV exhibited sharp styling from every angle. With a new, longer frame and a completely new body, it incorporated many features of the successful Mark III, including the

Power for the Mark IV came from the same engine used in the Mark III: a 460 cu.in. big-block V8 that was rated at 212 horsepower; an engine also used in the Continental sedan. The Mark IV also shared the sedan's drive-train and coil-spring suspension.

It was an immediate success; the Mark III had sold well against the Eldorado, but the Mark IV outsold it, and continued to do so for the next two years. The car's popularity generated intense owner loyalty, many remaining with the same owners for years, providing a degree of luxury and style that American manufacturers eventually ceased to offer.

The Mark IV would remain in production until 1976 but, as the years passed, exhaust emissions equipment would strangle the engine and heavy energy-absorbing bumpers would add to the car's weight, reducing performance. Even so, the Mark IV remained a winner until the end. Production peaked at 69,437 in 1973, and reached 56,110 in 1976, indicating just how popular the car was.

Above: For 1972, Chrysler continued with the "fuselage" styling introduced in 1969, as this New Yorker Brougham 4-door hardtop illustrates. The smooth rounded sides accentuated the car's length, while a massive expanse of hood did the same for its width.

Below: Ford restyled its dual-purpose, car-based pickup, the Ranchero, for 1972, adopting the Coke-bottle shape that was prevalent in standard automobiles at the time. As always, the Ranchero provided the comfort of a car with the load-carrying ability of a truck, but its days were numbered by the arrival of the much cheaper Japanese mini-trucks that had almost as much load space.

large chromed grille, fold-away head lights and the Continental spare hump on the trunk. The Mark III had sold well, but the Mark IV did even better, outselling the rival Cadillac Eldorado for the first time.

1973

By just about any yardstick, 1973 wasn't exactly a vintage year – although the signing of the Vietnam War cease-fire agreement on January 27th seemed to indicate that there was some cause for optimism. Unfortunately, the aftermath of the Watergate break-in was about to engulf The White House and both President Nixon and Vice President Spiro Agnew resigned following a tax evasion scandal. And, if this upheaval wasn't demoralizing enough, there was the oil crisis caused by the OPEC embargo which resulted in long queues at gas stations. The automobile industry was further hampered by the imposition of a nationwide 55mph speed limit.

Given those circumstances, it would seem unlikely that a car born in the youth-driven Sixties – when performance was everything and fuel economy didn't matter – could even survive, let alone nearly double its sales. But the Pontiac Firebird has always been a rather special automobile and, anyway, nobody ever said there was much logic in the reasons people had for choosing which car to buy.

In many respects, it is actually quite remarkable that there was a '73 Firebird at all, given the situation in 1972. Pontiac faced problems on several fronts, the most damaging for the Firebird line being a five month-long strike by the United Auto Workers union at the Norwood, Ohio plant where the cars were built. By the time the stoppage ended in September, the losses amounted to thousands of cars representing millions of dollars that the company could ill-afford. With the situation as it was, there is little wonder that there was considerable pressure from the GM boardroom to drop the model from the catalog altogether.

Further complications arose from the increased number of Federal safety regulations being introduced and the power-sapping emission control systems required – all of which tended to work against the pony car brigade. It was as if the fun had been taken out of driving and, as a result, many of the cars being produced lost their individuality as the design and engineering teams struggled to incorporate the new changes dictated by legislation.

It is no surprise to learn, therefore, that the '73 Firebird showed few obvious alterations from the previous year. Well, unless you look at the hood of the Trans Am that is! Nobody

could possibly miss that huge "screaming chicken" decal which has since become the enduring symbol of the Firebird. The idea for the gigantic stick-on had originally come from chief designer Bill Porter and his assistant Wayne Vieira for a pair of show cars being prepared in 1970. However, GM's tyrannical head of styling, Bill Mitchell, took an instant dislike to the big bird and put a stop to it being used.

Bill Porter was promoted in '71 and in his place came young designer, John Schinella, who set about resurrecting the huge hood motif and managed to persuade Mitchell to accept it. Schinella redesigned the decal so it differed from the smaller version that had appeared on the nose of earlier cars and the Porter/Vieria design that Mitchell objected to. The name of the artist responsible for the very first rendition of the Firebird logo remains unknown, simply for the fact that it was copied from a mural on the wall at the airport of Phoenix, Arizona! But that initial design was far more traditional in execution and was only used as a small decorative feature on the fenders and rear of '68 and '69 models.

For a model that started out in 1967 as basically a Chevrolet Camaro with a nose job and a different rear end, the Firebird quickly developed its own separate identity, partly

Above: The Pontiac Firebird Trans Am came bedecked with spoilers, air dams, scoops and flares for '73, but in its best form – the SD-455 – it was capable of over 130mph and could handle corners well too. However, its braking capability was deemed to be rather marginal for such a high performance car.

thanks to some clever styling work – initially by Pontiac's head of design, Jack Humbert, followed by Bill Porter. Skillful engineering of the suspension and drivetrain, and the use of Pontiac's own range of engines helped to establish this identity all the more. However, the Pontiac powerplants did face one draw back when it came to calling the model, Trans Am, after the race series of the same name – the V8s were all of too big a capacity to run in the championship.

The highly successful Trans Am series was organised by the Sports Car Club of America (SCCA) and, in the 1960s, it attracted a lot of media attention and factory-backed entries of Ford Mustangs, Chevy Camaros, Mercury Cougars, AMC Javelins and others.

Right: The Trans Am's giant "screaming chicken" hood decal appeared for the first time in '73 and quickly became the trademark of all Firebird models. Designer John Schinella was responsible for getting the motif approved by GM's head of styling Bill Mitchell.

But the 303 cu.in. maximum limit on engine size presented Pontiac with a problem in that their smallest production V8 displaced 350 cu.in. In a bid to get round the regulations, Pontiac co-operated with the T/G Racing Team of Jerry Titus and Terry Godsall who entered "Canadian" Firebirds (actually Camaros with Pontiac front sheet metal) equipped with Chevy 302 cu.in. engines. After a while, Pontiac produced a special destroked version of the 400 cu.in. engine and managed to convince SCCA officials that

this was going into series production, and so allowing them entry to the series. However, with this hurdle overcome, winning was to prove elusive.

As it happened, track success wasn't necessary for the Firebird Trans Am to be triumphant on the street and, after its low key introduction in '69, the model went on to evolve into a great American sports car. Bedecked with spoilers, air dams, hood scoops and flares, the Trans Am looked just like a race car should, and handled better

Right: The first major styling change to the Sting Ray came in '73 but the rear view of the Chevy didn't look much different from previous years. The famed LT1 high performance engine was dropped, and new top spec was a 454 cu.in. LS4 that produced 275bhp.

Below: The Sting Ray had urethane plastic covers over steel bumpers to comply with federally mandated "5mph" bumpers. The extra two inches in length was more acceptable than the 35 pounds in weight. Extra insulation reduced noise as the Corvette became more of a long-distance freeway cruiser.

than most of the competition too. From 1971 onwards, the only engine available was the 455 cu.in. V8 and, if by '73 its power had been strangled down to a meek-sounding 290 horsepower for the optional Super Duty version (250hp was standard), there was still sufficient "grunt" to give some seat-of-the-pants excitement when the right hand pedal was pushed to the floor in anger.

Exactly how well the people at Pontiac had preserved the Trans Am's performance in the face of the ever-increasing restrictive legislation can be judged by contemporary road test reports. Hot Rod magazine cranked out a 13.54 second quarter mile at 104 mph, while Car & Driver were only a fraction slower at 13.75 secs and 103 mph. These were impressive numbers by any standards, and Car & Driver also made the point that the '73 Trans Am was actually quicker than the 1970 version with 340 horsepower on tap. It is no wonder that the SD-455 has become something of a legend among Firebird enthusiasts ever since.

And it wasn't just the car's capability to go fast in a straight line that C&D liked; the Trans

Am was just as quick off the mark when going round corners: "...the Trans Am's second most endearing quality – next to its ability to out-accelerate anything not assisted by a rocket motor – is handling". They were less than happy with the brakes on a car timed at 132 mph though, and suggested that the semi-metallic front brake pads from the heavy duty Police Package were a must. The report concluded: "The Firebird Trans Am is a genus of an automotive species approaching extinction. It could be the last of its kind. Just the car you need to carry you through the upcoming years of automotive sterility..." With the benefit of hindsight, perhaps it is only now that we can fully appreciate that this statement was really quite an amazing piece of prophetic writing.

The 1973 Pontiac Firebird Trans Am was virtually the final fling of the mass produced, cheap, high performance car for a couple of decades. And, even over twenty years later, it remains as an exceptional example of just how good an American sports coupe can be, no matter what obstacles are imposed by the law makers.

Above: In '73, full-sized cars like this Ford LTD 2-door hard top were pretty hefty animals, stretching to over 17 feet long and tipping the scales at nearly two tons. In retrospect, it's hard to believe that LTD was voted Car of the Year by Road Test magazine, but with over 941,000 full-size Custom/Galaxie/LTD models sold in 1973, there were obviously plenty of willing customers.

1974

In politics, 1974 was a year of change. Watergate had finally caught up with Richard Nixon, who resigned from the Presidency on 8th August. His replacement, Vice President Gerald Ford, pardoned him a month later.

Another event of that year was the kidnapping of heiress Patty Hearst, who promptly joined her kidnappers to take part in a bank robbery. There was violence in Boston over the bussing of black students; and pioneer aviator Charles Lindbergh died.

There was good news on the automotive front in that OPEC had lifted their oil embargo of the United States, but sadly it came too late to save the big-bodied, big-engined, gas-guzzling American automobile that so many had come to love. Faced with stringent exhaust emissions regulations and the rising price of gasoline, Detroit had no choice but to turn its back on the type of cars it had traditionally built. Intermediate models, compacts and sub-compacts with cleaner, smaller, more economical engines were the order of the day. While many of them would prove to be efficient, none would ever have the guts, glitz and sheer personality of what had gone before. The new 1974 models heralded the end of the truly individual American automobile, and America would not see its like again.

Above: Engine-wise, the top Road Runner option for 1974 was the four-barrel-equipped 440 cu.in. V8 that delivered 280 horsepower. The capacity of the engine was lettered on the hood, while bold stripes were applied to the sides and roof pillars. The 440 engine came with an automatic transmission only.

Left: The "fuselage" styling of the Satellite body certainly looked right for a muscle car, but by now those looks were more important than the raw power such cars used to deliver.

spectacular successes in NASCAR and drag racing helped boost sales. Included in the Dodge Scat Pack and Plymouth Rapid Transit System were the Dodge Super Bee and Charger, and the Plymouth GTX and Road Runner. But, by 1974, strangled by emissions equipment and dogged by high running costs, such cars were no longer selling well.

Typical of these Chrysler products was the Plymouth Road Runner. Based on the "fuselage-styled" Satellite body shell, it came with a 170 horsepower small-block 318 cu.in. V8 as standard, which had replaced its previous 400 cu.in. big-block engine in 1973. For the first time on the Road Runner, the engine was fitted with a two-barrel carburetor. The normal transmission was a three-speed manual, although a four-speed and automatic were options. Also optional were 360, 400 and 440 cu.in. engines.

By now, looks were more important than power, and the car sported bold contrasting stripes that curved down from the rear roof pillars and along the waist line to the front edges of the front fenders. Its looks may have promised more than its standard drivetrain could deliver but, nevertheless, it was the last true Road Runner. In 1975, it would be based on the small Fury, and after that merely an options package for the Volare.

From 1919 to 1974, Detroit built many great, intriguing and memorable automobiles. Fortunately, today there are enthusiasts worldwide who cherish examples of those wonderful cars. Through them, generations to come will be able to enjoy the sights and sounds of the Great American Automobile.

Above: The shape of things to come. Ford's original muscle car, the Mustang, had already been transformed into its new, "more respectable" form. Mustang II was down in size, down on power and down in charisma. Some of the original styling cues were still there – the protruding grille, the side moldings and the running horse emblem – but it was not enough to give the car the raw excitement of the original. Nor were the engines: a 140 cu.in. overhead-cam four and a 171 cu.in. V6. In time, Mustang II would receive a V8 and various trim packages to make it look more aggressive but, even then, it would never match the car that started the race.

The muscle cars which had appeared with the Mustang a decade before were among the casualties. Some had already ceased production, while the rest would not linger for long.

Chrysler, through its Dodge and Plymouth divisions, had been a major contender in the muscle car wars for some years, building a range of machines based on its intermediate models. These were real fire-breathing street-'n'-strip monsters: no-frills quarter-mile machines with powerful engines, four-speed manual transmissions, and beefed-up rear ends and suspensions. The engines included the awesome 425 horsepower 426 hemi V8 and the 390 horsepower 440 Six Pack engine, equipped with three two-barrel carburetors. The no-frills approach allowed Chrysler to price them for the younger market, while

Index

Acknowledgements

The publishers would like to thank the following for their kind loan or supply of photographs for this book:

Courtesy of Ford Motor Company
page 8/9 top, 29 top, 38, 42 bottom, 51 bottom, 64/5 top, 88/9 bottom, 96/7 bottom, 114/5 bottom, 120 bottom, 135, 144/5 top, 156, 157 bottom, 160 top, 172/3 top, 175, 180 top, 182/3 top left and bottom left, 183 bottom, 187, 189 right

General Motors Corp., used with permission
page 9 bottom, 25 bottom right, 34/5 bottom, 58 bottom, 72, 73 top, 82/3 bottom, 87 top, 124/5 bottom, 131 bottom right, 133 bottom, 134, 152 bottom, 153, 162/3 top, 173 bottom, 178/9 top

Courtesy Oldsmobile History Center
page 15, 43 bottom, 70, 71 bottom, 79 top, 109, 120/1 top left, 137 top, 140/1 top, 157 top, 160 bottom, 172 bottom

Free Library of Philadelphia
page 1, 8 bottom, 12, 16/7 bottom, 18 top, 18/9 center, 20 center, 20/1 top and bottom, 26 bottom, 30, 31, 32 bottom, 36/7 bottom, 42/3 top left, 48/9 bottom, 52, 53, 55 bottom, 85 top, 63 bottom, 66 bottom, 78, 86, 98 top, 152 top, 183 top, back of jacket (bottom)

Studebaker National Museum
page 80/1 bottom, 81 top

IMS Photos, Indianapolis Motor Speedway
page 13 bottom, 14 bottom, 23 top, 56, 99, 112/3 top, 141 bottom, 158 bottom

Chrysler Historical Collection
page 146, 154/5 top and center

National Motor Museum, Beaulieu
page 13 top, 14 top, 17 top, 19 right, 21 top right, 22/3 bottom, 25 top, 27 bottom, 32/3 top, 34 top, 35 right, 36/7 top, 39 top, 40/1 bottom, 43 top right, 45 right, 46 bottom, 46/7 top, 50 bottom, 54 bottom, 57, 60/1 left, 62, 65 bottom, 66/7 top, 74, 90 top, 98 bottom, 100 bottom, 116, 131 top, 138/9 bottom, 140 bottom, 144 bottom, 145 bottom, 161, 164 top, 166/7 bottom, 168/9 bottom, 170/1 bottom

Tony Beadle Collection
page 25 left, 26/7 top, 35 top right, 75 bottom, 76/7 bottom, 79

bottom, 100/1 top, 110, 111, 113 bottom, 123 bottom, 148 bottom, 149, 150, 151, 163 bottom, 171 top, front of jacket

The Advertising Archive
page 28 top, 33 bottom, 48 top, 63 top, 75 top, 80 top, 96 top

Nicky Wright/National Motor Museum, Beaulieu
page 37 top right, 47 bottom, 82 top, 87 bottom, 121 bottom, 124 top, 137 bottom, 148 top, 158/9 top, 177, 179 bottom

Nicky Wright, Marshall, Michigan, USA
page 10, 11, 22 top, 41 top right, 44, 64 bottom, 83 top, 84/5 top, 114/5 top, 136 top, 143 bottom, 176, 181 right, 184, 185, 188 bottom, 188/9 center

Mike Key
page 68, 69, 73 bottom, 94, 102, 103, 104 top, 117 bottom, 118, 119, 127 bottom, 128, 129, 147, 169 top, 186

Dan Lyons
page 54/5 top, 92, 93, 101 bottom, 105, 112 bottom, 117 top, 142/3 top, 164 bottom, 165, 168 top

Andrew Morland
page 28/9 bottom, 40/1 top left, 50/1 top, 59, 61 right, 122 bottom, 122/3 top

William D. Siuru
page 4/5, 24, 67 bottom, 71 top, 77 top, 84 bottom, 85 bottom, 90 bottom, 91, 121 top right, 126/7 top, 130, 138/9 top, 154 bottom, 180 bottom

Jim Maxwell
page 2/3, 6/7, 159 bottom, 162 bottom

Anders Odeholm, The Media Factory AB
page 108, 167 top

Colin Burnham
page 95, 132/3 top, 136 bottom

Rob Sargent
endpapers, back of jacket (top)

Julian Balme
page 106, 107

Rod Blackaller
page 174

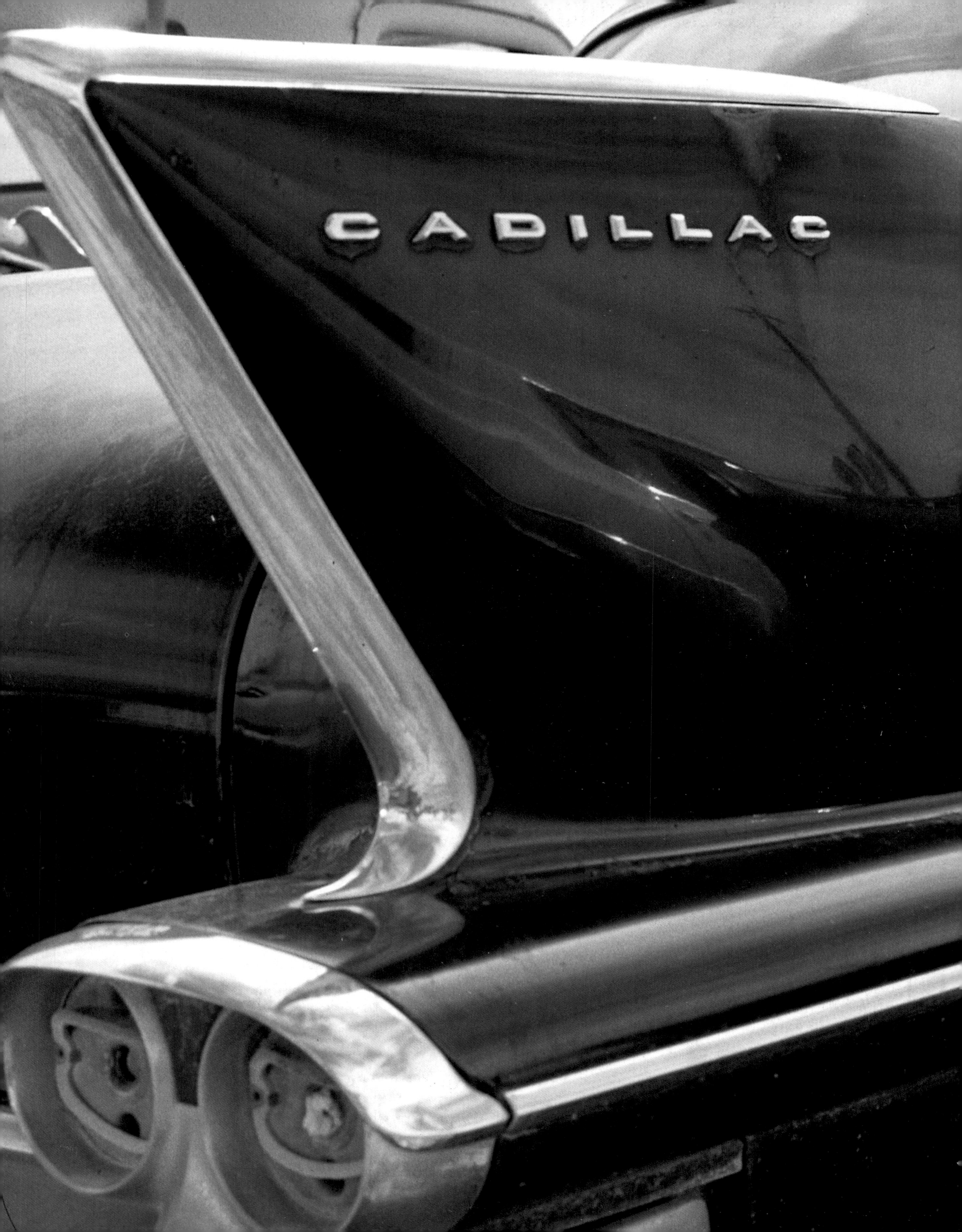
CADILLAC